CULTURE SHOCK!
Canada

**Pang Guek Cheng
& Robert Barlas**

Graphic Arts Center Publishing Company
Portland, Oregon

In the same series

Australia
Borneo
Britain
China
France
Indonesia
Israel
Malaysia
Nepal
Pakistan
Philippines
Sri Lanka
Thailand
USA

Forthcoming

Burma
India
Italy
Japan
Korea
Singapore
Spain

Illustrations by John Mortimer
Photographs by Bill Murtha,
Bob Barlas and Pang Guek Cheng
Cover photographs by courtesy of
British Columbia Ministry of Tourism

© 1992 Times Editions Pte Ltd

This book is published by special
arrangement with Times Editions Pte Ltd
International Standard Book Number 1-55868-087-X
Library of Congress Catalog Number 91-077243
Graphic Arts Center Publishing Company
P.O. Box 10306 • Portland, Oregon 97210 • (503) 226-2402

Printed in Singapore by Chong Moh Offset Printing Pte Ltd

CONTENTS

To my wife Nancy, my son Richard, my daughter Sharine,
and Ann and Ivor Davies

To Pius, always my inspiration, and my children,
Christopher and Gerardine

ACKNOWLEDGEMENTS

When we first met each other, we remarked upon the happy chance that we were indeed 'opposites' – Caucasian and male, long-term resident of eastern Canada complementing Asian and female, a newcomer to western Canada – and could bring different viewpoints to *Culture Shock! Canada*. Since then, many hours of cross-Canada telephone time have gone into the creation of this book, and a friendship has been formed. What we lacked ourselves, we supplemented with information solicited from many sources and with suggestions from our own friends.

Writing this book has therefore placed us in debt to a large number of people, and when trying to deal with such a huge topic as the entire country of Canada, the list of those who helped must necessarily be even larger than usual. To all of you who made contributions in one way or another – from suggestions on the myriad of topics covered in *Culture Shock! Canada* to simply expressing interest in our project – thank you for your support.

Special thanks must go, however, to those who so ably helped us research the facts which we needed to make this book accurate:

From Bob: to Robert Amesse, Elizabeth Mitchell and Norm Tompsett – first-class librarians all – to Denise Maxfield, Mike Filip, and Jim and Joanne Rich, whose contributions to various parts of the text were invaluable, and to Vern Shute and Charles Clarke, who proofread my text with great accuracy and precision. Finally, especial gratitude to my good friends Bill Murtha and John Mortimer, whose artistic suggestions and contributions helped immensely in visualising the text as it was being written.

From Guek Cheng: thanks especially to Shirley Hew and Shova Loh who made me an author; to John Bartle, Mark Looi and Diane Quinn, for their invaluable help; to Bob and Clare Looi, who introduced me to this beautiful country; and to my new-found Canadian friends too numerous to name individually, but who have welcomed me into their midst.

Both of us wish to thank Times Editions who have been more than supportive of the project, and for this most of the credit must go to our editor, Roseline Lum, and to the series editor, Shova Loh, for their help and encouragement.

Last, but by no means least, our gratitude and love to our families whose constructive criticism and moral support have been invaluable during the weeks and months it took to put this book together. We have both learnt more about the country we live in by writing *Culture Shock! Canada* – and we hope that you, the reader, will share the enthusiasm for the country which has gone into these pages.

Robert Barlas
Pang Guek Cheng
December 1991

Chapter One

THIS LAND IS MY LAND

'Humongous' is a Canadian word that is an apt description for the country. Here are some facts to give you an idea of what it means:

- Canada's width from the Atlantic to the Pacific is more than 7700 kilometres, more than four times the width of India. It would take a good two weeks to drive across the country from coast to coast.
- From its southernmost point, where Pelee Island rises out of Lake Erie, to Ellesmere Island in the Arctic Ocean, Canada is about 4800 kilometres, or more than five times the length of Japan.
- All in all, Canada covers nearly 10 million square kilometres in area. It is the second largest country in the world. It is larger than

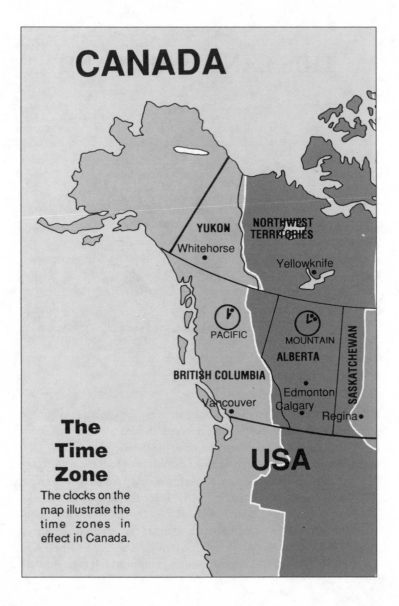

CANADA

YUKON

Whitehorse •

NORTHWEST TERRITORIES

Yellowknife •

PACIFIC

MOUNTAIN

ALBERTA

SASKATCHEWAN

BRITISH COLUMBIA

Vancouver •

Edmonton •
Calgary •

Regina •

The Time Zone

The clocks on the map illustrate the time zones in effect in Canada.

USA

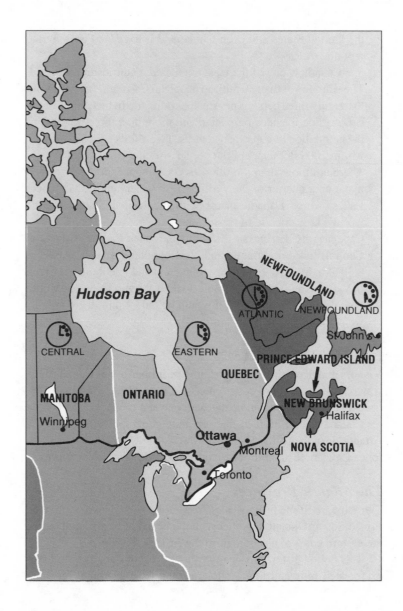

the United States and even China, and is exceeded only by the republic of Russia.

- Yet Canada is one of the least populated countries in the world. There are fewer than 30 million people in Canada. That works out to roughly three persons per square kilometre. In fact, much of the countryside is under-populated and more than three-quarters of the population live in urban centres. Two-thirds are concentrated within 200 kilometres of the border with the United States.
- There are more than a million rivers, streams and lakes, which make up a quarter of the world's fresh water supply. The Great Lakes, which Canada shares with the United States, are the world's largest body of fresh water.
- Canada is divided into six different time zones: Pacific, Mountain, Central, Eastern, Atlantic and Newfoundland. If you arrived at 8.30 a.m. in St John's in Newfoundland and telephoned a friend in Vancouver, British Columbia, to relay the good news, he would probably be fast asleep as it would be only 4 a.m. there and his welcome might be lukewarm!

FROM SEA TO SEA

Visitors may have difficulty grasping the immensity of Canada. One way of making it more comprehensible is to divide it into smaller, 'bite-size' pieces that can be digested one at a time.

Canada can be divided into six main geographical regions: the Atlantic Provinces, the Canadian Shield, the Great Lakes-St Lawrence Lowlands, the Interior Plains, the Cordillera and the North.

The Atlantic Provinces

The three maritime provinces of New Brunswick, Nova Scotia and Prince Edward Island, together with the island of Newfoundland on the eastern coast of Canada, form the Atlantic Provinces.

This region differs physically from the rest of Canada because of its forested hills and low mountains, and its rugged and indented coast. These physical characteristics have resulted in separating the people of this region into small communities and scattering their settlements. Therefore there are few areas of high population density in the Atlantic Provinces.

The provinces are a cluster of peninsulas and islands which form the northeastern extension of the Appalachian Highlands and are greatly affected by the Atlantic Ocean. They are home to only about 10% of the country's population and have always been the poorest provinces of Canada. The main industries are resource-based, relying on fishing and forestry. Often the economy and survival of a whole town can depend on a single industry.

The Canadian Shield

The Canadian Shield is an enormous area that occupies about half of the mainland of Canada. It is made up of the northern half of Manitoba, Ontario, Quebec and Labrador (the mainland part of the province of Newfoundland).

The Canadian Shield, also known as the Pre-Cambrian or Laurentian Shield, was formed more than 2 billion years ago. This ancient, glacially eroded region is full of rivers, lakes and forests, making it a hunter's and fisherman's paradise. Practically uninhabit-able, the Canadian Shield is responsible for keeping Canadians closely hemmed in to the border with the United States, and accounts for the physical separation of eastern and western Canada. But the area is rich in resources, producing 40% of Canada's minerals – cobalt, copper, gold, iron, nickel, silver, uranium and zinc – and wood. Canada is one of the two major pulp and paper producers in the world. The Canadian Shield's other great resource is water, supplying the area further south, the lowlands of the St Lawrence, with 70% of its electricity (hydroelectricity or 'hydro-power').

The Great Lakes and St Lawrence Lowlands

This very small area of Canada extends across the south of the two provinces of Ontario and Quebec. Despite its size, it is here that more than half of Canada's population lives. This densely-populated part of eastern Canada contains more large cities of over 100,000 people than any other part of Canada of similar size. The metropolitan centres of Montreal, Quebec City, Toronto and Ottawa are all situated here.

This area includes the heartland of French Canada; yet there are also strongholds of British settlement. Some of the contrasts of the land are due to cultural differences between French and Anglo-Saxon patterns of settlement.

The rich agricultural land, once all cultivated, attracted many settlers in the 18th and 19th centuries, but much of it has now become a great urban and industrial area. This region produces about three-quarters of all the country's manufactured goods in an area known as the Quebec-Windsor corridor, which stretches between those two cities and along the shores of the St Lawrence River and Lake Ontario. Another factor making this the richest part of the country is the great waterway formed by the St Lawrence River and the Great Lakes. This waterway is ice-free for most of the year, thus giving the inland region around it access to the Atlantic Ocean and the rest of the world.

The Interior Plains or the Prairies

This region can be simply described with one word – flat. This part of Canada is roughly made up of the central provinces of Alberta, Saskatchewan and the southern part of Manitoba. It is bounded on the west by the Rockies and on the east by the Canadian Shield. The plains are flat and, as you travel by train through it, level as far as the eye can see. This region has always been, and still is, Canada's 'bread basket'. Half of its area is forested and most of the other half is devoted to the growing of grain, especially wheat, making Canada the second largest exporter of grain in the world behind the United States.

A quarter of the population in the prairies is made up of immigrants from Germany, Eastern Europe, the Ukraine and Russia, whose ancestors transformed the barren plain into today's fertile

A spectacular waterfall in the Canadian Rockies.

farmland. The domes of Russian and Greek Orthodox churches are especially visible in this region. The Métis, of mixed French and Indian ancestry, form a small but significant part of the population.

The Cordillera

This mountainous region starts from the Rockies in the east. It consists of plateaux and valleys in the middle and ends with another mountainous range along the edge of the Pacific Ocean in the west. It corresponds roughly to the political divisions of British Columbia, the Yukon and part of Alberta.

Great contrasts can be seen in this region – there are the English gardens of Victoria, the wilderness of the Rockies, the rolling hills and plateaux of the interior and the coastal forests. Most of the population is concentrated in the south and near the coast, where the main cities of Vancouver and Victoria are located. Forestry and the paper and pulp industry, cattle and other animal farming are vital to the population in the interior of British Columbia. This is easily one of the most scenic parts of Canada, rivalled only by the mountains of the Northwest Territories. The spectacular scenery has made tourism an important industry in British Columbia.

The Great White North

Comprising the Northwest Territories and the Yukon, this region covers about 40% of Canada's land area. Much of it is cold, isolated and almost entirely uninhabited. About 17,000 of the world's Inuit population live here. (Inuit means 'the people', a name they prefer over Eskimos, which means 'meat-eaters'). Another native people in the far North are the Dene Indians (Dene also means 'the people'). A third people are the Métis, who trace their ancestry to the unions between the French *coureurs de bois* and Indian women in the early days of the fur trade. A mainly transient community of adventurers, hunters, trappers, missionaries, people who work for the mining, oil and other natural resource industries and their support services make up the remainder of the people who inhabit this great white land.

The native communities are located on bays, river mouths and inlets, reflecting their basic lifestyle of hunting, fishing and gathering.

Biologists divide the North into two regions: the boreal forest and the tundra. The boreal forest is a broad band of coniferous forest extending across Canada from Newfoundland to Alaska. The tundra, which reaches from the boreal forest northwards to the Arctic Ocean, comprises 20% of Canada's landmass. It is treeless. The two regions meet along the tree line, a transitional zone several kilometres wide. This boundary also separates the traditional lands of the Indians and the Inuit. The Inuit occupy the shores of the Arctic Ocean and of the Hudson Bay, the Indians the Yukon and the Mackenzie Valley.

Looking at it another way, the region can be sub-divided into the sub-arctic Mackenzie River valley in the west and the arctic area of the northern islands and the north-central mainland.

In the middle of summer, it is never dark in the North. And in mid-winter, the only daylight is a combination of sunset and sunrise. Summers can be pleasantly warm with temperatures rising above 20°C but the season is short and often wet. Rainfall and snowfall are light because the Arctic is really semi-desert. Yet the ground is often wet and swampy because there is a layer of ground below the surface that is permanently frozen. When the snow thaws, the water remains on the surface and cannot drain through the frozen ground.

Mineral resources are the economic mainstay of this region, but the forbidding climate and extreme isolation of the area make exploitation of the land difficult. Nevertheless, it is non-renewable resources like gold, silver, lead, zinc, copper, oil and natural gas that have spurred the economic development of the North. These industries do not produce widespread permanent settlement, but rather promote the rise of 'instant' towns with labour imported from the south. A large part of the white population in the North is transient in nature. Even government employees regard their time in the North as just a 'tour of duty' limited to several years.

Tourism is a short-term, basically summer industry. Visitors come mainly from the United States and the southern parts of Canada to view nature's breathtaking and unspoiled beauty – the treeless landscape, alpine scenery, ice floes, icebergs and glaciers, and the mountains of Baffin, Devon and Ellesmere islands which are the highest in eastern North America.

REGIONAL QUIRKS AND QUARKS

Politically, Canada is made up of 10 provinces and two northern territories. The provinces, from east to west, are Newfoundland, Nova Scotia, Prince Edward Island, New Brunswick, Quebec, Ontario, Manitoba, Saskatchewan, Alberta and British Columbia. They have their own governments which are primarily responsible for public schooling, health and social services, highways and local government. The two northern territories are the Northwest Territories and the Yukon. The territories are governed by the federal government in Ottawa and by territorial governments which may legislate where the federal government has given it the necessary authority.

Newfoundland

Total land area: 393,173 km^2
Total fresh water area: 34,030 km^2
Coastline: 19,720 km
Population (1989): 571,000 (2.18% of total Canadian population)
Capital: St John's
International airport: Gander

Newfoundland (pronounced 'newf-n-land') is the furthest east of the Canadian provinces. The main part of the province is the island of Newfoundland, which has a mountainous and lake-strewn interior and a rocky, rugged coastline. There are few big cities, and life is mainly centred around small fishing communities on the coast, known as 'outports'. These 'outports' are dispersed along the coast in

sheltered bays, near headlands or on islands, and even today, there are some that are only accessible by boat. These are mainly along the south coast where no road linking them has been built yet. The isolation of these villages means that today's way of life and culture have not changed much since the arrival of the early settlers from Europe. Cars are a luxury, but who needs them here anyway? Access to the 'outports' is difficult. Some are on ferry lines, others are not. These little communities are some of the most remote settlements in North America.

Labrador, the mainland portion of the province, is mainly wild and sparsely populated. Many of the communities in this region are extremely isolated and travel is commonly accomplished on water. Newfoundlanders (or 'Newfies' as they are sometimes referred to by other Canadians) are mainly descended from British immigrants. They have a very distinct culture, most noticeable in their language, which is full of colourful and unique slang and idioms. Some words which cannot be heard in any other part of the country are 'ballycater' (a narrow band of ice which forms along the foreshore in winter), 'kinkhorn' (the throat or windpipe), 'sparbles' (shoemaker's nails) and 'yaffle' (to gather in a pile). Also unique is the fact that the island of Newfoundland has no snakes or skunks.

Fishing is the main occupation of Newfoundlanders. Other industries are mining, hydroelectricity and forestry. The weather is cool throughout the year, with the moderating influence of the sea reduced by the cold waters of the Labrador Current. Winters are mild and summers cool and short. It is relatively wet.

St John's is the capital of the province and its largest town. It combines the feel of a high-rise city and a coastal fishing village. It is also the oldest city in North America and England's first overseas colony, the very beginnings of the British Empire.

Access to Newfoundland from the mainland by ferry is from North Sydney, Nova Scotia. There is a year-round service to Port aux Basques and a seasonal service to Argentia on the Avalon Peninsula.

Nova Scotia

Total land area: 55,491 km^2
Total fresh water area: 2650 km^2
Coastline: 5934 km
Population (1989): 885,900 (3.38% of total Canadian population)
Capital: Halifax
International airport: Halifax

Nova Scotia is very much like Newfoundland, and as it is a peninsular province, no part is too far from the sea. The climate is wet and cold, but the summers and winters here are more moderate than in areas of the same latitude in the interior of the country. Winters may be stormy, however, and there is a problem with fog all year round. The rugged coastline is cut by numerous bays and inlets, ideal sites for fishing villages. The catch includes cod, lobster and scallops. However, the main industry is manufacturing, along with shipbuilding, and the production of dairy goods and paper. Scenically, the mountainous landscapes of the Cape Breton Highlands, which jut out to the north, contrast with the relatively flat agricultural land which lies around the south of the peninsula. An area with a difference is the beautiful Annapolis Valley, along the Bay of Fundy, which is famous for its apples and is most beautiful in spring when pink and white apple blossoms cover the trees.

The population is mainly of English and Scottish ancestry, but there are French, German and Dutch communities scattered throughout the province. Nova Scotia means 'New Scotland', and the Scottish influence is strong everywhere, especially in Cape Breton in the north. Highland games are a highlight of the summer months. In some areas, you can still hear Gaelic being spoken.

Due to its favourable position on the Atlantic, Nova Scotia has always been strategically important. Halifax, with a population of about 120,000, is the capital of the province and the largest city in the maritime provinces. It is the headquarters of Canada's small navy and a major port owing to its year-round accessibility.

Prince Edward Island
Total land area: 5656 km^2
Total fresh water area: None
Coastline: 1107 km
Population (1989): 130,000 (0.5% of total Canadian population)
Capital: Charlottetown
International airport: None

Prince Edward Island is the smallest province of Canada and the most densely populated. Its rich, red soil supports a mainly farming community that produces potatoes as the main crop. Fishing – for lobsters, oysters and herring – is also important. The warm ocean currents that wash the Gulf of St Lawrence where the island lies give Prince Edward Island a climate that is much warmer than most of Canada. But the island is also wet and there are occasional extreme low temperatures in winter.

Charlottetown, an old, quiet country town with a population of about 45,000, was named by its Loyalist settlers after Queen Charlotte, the consort of George III. It claims to be the 'Cradle of Confederation', site of the historic meeting which took place in 1864 and which eventually led to the unification of Canada in 1867.

Prince Edward Island is only accessible by ferry from the mainland. There are two services: a continuous service which runs year round from Cape Tormentine, New Brunswick, and a seasonal service from Caribou, Nova Scotia.

New Brunswick

Total land area: 73,437 km^2
Total fresh water area: 1350 km^2
Coastline: 1524 km
Population (1989): 718,600 (2.74% of total Canadian population)
Capital: Fredericton
International airport: None

New Brunswick is rectangular in shape and has an extensive sea coast. The proximity of the sea has a moderating influence on a climate that has mostly cool summers and cold winters. The land is covered with forests; the wooded highlands are cut by many fast rivers and deep valleys. As can be expected, forestry and pulp and paper are the two main industries.

The descendants of the Acadian French settlers make up a sizeable part of the population, as do descendants of the United Empire Loyalists who migrated north at the time of the American War of Independence.

Fredericton, the province's capital, was named for the second son of George III. It is a quiet tree-lined city which retains the grace and dignity brought to it by its Loyalist founders. Many old buildings and elegant houses remain. Fredericton is the home of the province's lieutenant-governor and its legislature.

Strange formations abound in the sea-eroded flowerpot rocks at Hopewell Cape, jutting out into the Bay of Fundy.

An interesting spectacle is the 'bore tide' on the Bay of Fundy, which New Brunswick shares with Nova Scotia. When the incoming tide reaches its peak, it creates a wall of water which roars all at once into the towns of Moncton, New Brunswick, and Truro, Nova Scotia. This surge of water occurs twice a day and the exact times are predicted in advance. Special viewing platforms are provided for visitors to watch its arrival. A similar phenomenon occurs in St John, New Brunswick, when rushing water up the St John River creates 'reversing falls', in reality a series of rapids which appear to change direction under the pressure of the incoming tide. Another New Brunswick geographical oddity is the 'Magnetic Hill' near Moncton, on which cars appear to coast backwards without any power – uphill!

Quebec
Total land area: 1,540,687 km^2

Total fresh water area: 183,890 km^2
Coastline: 10,839 km
Population (1989): 6,692,100 (25.52% of total Canadian population)
Capital: Quebec City
International airports: Mirabel, Dorval (Montreal)

Quebec got its name from *kebec*, an Algonkian Indian word meaning 'where the river narrows'. Canada's largest province, almost half of it is forested. North of Montreal and Quebec City are the Laurentian Mountains. The area south of Montreal is mainly farmland. In the St Lawrence Valley, there is a long frost-free season from early May to September, but the northern and western parts of the province experience more extreme winter temperatures and cooler summers.

La belle province, as it is called, is the heart of French Canada. For many people, it is the existence of Quebec as a province that makes Canada unique. The mainly French population has a culture that makes it distinct from other parts of Canada, indeed the whole of North America. This is reflected in the language, architecture, music, food and religion of the region. For more than 85% of the people of Quebec, French is the mother tongue. Many of these *francophones* or Quebecois, as they are known, speak only French. About 90% of them are Roman Catholic. They tend to think of themselves more as Quebecois than as Canadians, and regard themselves as a different nation, though politically linked with the rest of Canada.

The countryside is rich in tradition and the remnants of the old 'seigneurial system' can still be seen in the layout of much of the countryside. The Gaspe region is a unique part of the province, an area of wild beauty where land ends in sheer cliffs falling into the Gulf of St Lawrence.

Quebec's wealth lies in its abundant natural resources. Nevertheless, it is manufacturing that is the main industry. Other important industries are aluminium, minerals and timber.

Montreal is Canada's second largest city, with a population of about 3 million people. About 12% of all Canadians and 40% of Quebecois live here. Two-thirds of the people are French-speaking, but the downtown core of the city is surprisingly English. Montreal is a major port and a centre for finance, business and transport. It is an arts centre as well, particularly for French Canada.

If Quebec is the heart of French Canada, then Quebec City is its heartbeat. The town is unique in many ways, but mostly in its European appearance and Old World atmosphere. The old section of town has been designated by UNESCO as a World Heritage Site. This is the seat of the provincial parliament and Laval University. Quebec City has been the centre of French nationalist thought for hundreds of years and today talk of independence and separatism is even more intense. The overwhelming majority of the people here are *francophones* (as opposed to *anglophones* who are more influenced by Anglo-Saxon language, thought and culture).

The climate is very changeable. Summers are fairly hot and not as long as in southern Ontario. Winter can get really cold, especially in January and February.

Ontario

Total land area: 1,068,587 km^2
Total fresh water area: 177,390 km^2
Coastline (on lakes): 1210 km
Population (1989): 9,578,700 (36.53% of total Canadian population)
Capital: Toronto
International airports: Pearson (Toronto), Ottawa

Ontario is a name derived from an Indian (Iroquois) word meaning 'rocks standing high near the water', which is probably a reference to the Niagara Falls.

It is by far the richest province, with about a third of all Canadians living here. Ethnically, it is also the most diverse. Here French and English are mixed with other European and Asian languages. The

A regular feature of Canada is the long winding river, as illustrated by this aerial picture of the northern Ontario landscape.

majority of the people are city dwellers and congregate in the area between Kingston and Windsor along the shores of the Great Lakes. The northern part of the province is, however, very under-populated. Most commercial activity is linked to the abundant natural resources – forestry and mining. The southern part of Ontario around the lakes has long, hot summers and mild winters, but it gets colder the further north you go into the province.

Manufacturing is the major industry. The cluster of cities around the western end of Lake Ontario is known as Canada's 'golden horseshoe'. It includes Hamilton (centre of Canada's iron and steel manufacture), Oshawa (centre of the automotive industry), Windsor (Detroit's twin city) and Toronto, Canada's largest city.

Toronto is the undisputed economic heart of the country, the nation's financial, business, publishing and fashion capital, and home to more than 200 of Canada's leading corporations. It is the centre for hundreds of suburbs and satellite towns and Canada's most ethnically diverse city – one of every four immigrants to Canada finds his way to Toronto. But despite its high-rise, big-city image, one of the most impressive things that usually strikes the visitor to Toronto is its cleanliness and orderliness. Much of the city is either new or has been rebuilt in the past 15 years. It has a reputation for being safe at night – the streets are busy, the restaurants and entertainment centres open, the parks and subways used in the way they are meant. There is none of the litter, graffiti and crime, no areas of concentrated poverty that can often be found in big cities. CN Tower, the tallest free-standing structure in the world (533 metres), is the city's symbol and landmark. At the top you can find a restaurant, a disco and two observation decks. Toronto is also the busiest Canadian port on the Great Lakes.

Besides Toronto, the attractions of Ontario include Ottawa, the country's capital, and the Niagara Falls, the tourist attraction which Canada shares with the United States.

Manitoba

Total land area: 650,090 km^2
Total fresh water area: 101,590 km^2
Length of coastline: 917 km
Population (1989): 1,084,800 (4.14% of total Canadian population)
Capital: Winnipeg
International airport: Winnipeg

The name Manitoba was derived from an Algonkian Indian word. In Lake Manitoba, there is a strait where the water makes an odd echoing sound which the Indians associated with Manito, the great spirit. So they named the place Manito Waba, meaning 'Manito Strait'.

The northern part of the province, which is part of the Canadian Shield, is hilly and forested, while the southern part is low and flat. The latter is ideal for farming, especially wheat, the province's most important crop. The main industry is manufacturing. Food processing and the clothing industry are also important. Winters are long and cold and summers can be hot.

Winnipeg, the capital, became the first stop of the great Canadian land rush of the late 19th century with the arrival of the Canadian Pacific Railroad. It is still home to the descendants of European immigrants who opened up the country – Ukrainians, Mennonites, Hungarians, Poles, Jews, Italians and Portuguese. Winnipeg grew into a railroad hub, the centre of the livestock and grain industry, and is the centre for grain handling and transport. It is the fourth largest city in Canada with a population of 650,000 people.

Saskatchewan
Total land area: 651,903 km^2
Total fresh water area: 81,632 km^2
Coastline: None
Population (1989): 1,007,300 (3.84% of total Canadian population)
Capital: Regina
International airport: None

Saskatchewan is a Cree Indian word meaning 'river that turns around when it runs'. This province produces two-thirds of Canada's wheat crop. Other grains grown are barley and rye. Oil and potash are Saskatchewan's most important resources. The province has the world's richest deposits of potash.

Two-thirds of Saskatchewan is very flat, prairie lowland, where there is often not a tree in sight. The climate is continental, with cold and long winters and warm and short summers.

Regina was originally dubbed 'Pile O'Bones' in reference to the bones left by the buffalo-hunting Indians who butchered their kill and left the remains here. It became the capital of the Northwest Territories and was the headquarters of the Northwest Mounted Police. Its name was changed to Regina (Latin for 'queen') in honour of Queen Victoria. In 1905, it became the capital of the newly-formed province of Saskatchewan. When oil and potash were discovered, Regina became the province's commercial, financial and industrial centre.

Saskatoon is the province's largest city (population 185,000). It was founded in 1882 by a group of Methodists from Ontario who were granted land to form a temperance colony. The coming of the railroad, combined with the resources of oil, potash and wheat, made Saskatoon one of Canada's fastest-growing cities.

Alberta

Total land area: 661,188 km^2
Total fresh water area: 16,796 km^2
Coastline: None
Population (1989): 2,423,000 (9.24% of total Canadian population)
Capital: Edmonton
International airports: Edmonton, Calgary

Alberta, the westernmost of the central provinces, is in the interior plains region. The south is subject in winter to the cold, dry air masses of the continental polar air, but summer is warm and full of sunshine.

Alberta came into its own in the 70s with the discovery of oil and natural gas. Besides these, Alberta also has other minerals, like coal, and agriculture is an important source of income.

The province is known as 'dinosaur country' as more dinosaur bones have been found here than anywhere else in the world. You can see the remains of dinosaurs in the south-central badlands and at the Dinosaur Provincial Park in the southeastern part of Alberta. The park was created in 1955 and has been declared a World Heritage Site.

Edmonton is the capital of Alberta and its largest city. It is known as the 'Gateway to the North' because it is situated on an economic divide between the highly productive farmlands of central Alberta and a vast resource-rich northern hinterland.

Calgary, the second largest city in Alberta, is strategically situated on major air, rail and road corridors, and is therefore an important transport centre. It is also the financial centre of western Canada and the headquarters of Canada's oil and natural gas industries.

British Columbia

Total land area: 948,601 km^2
Total fresh water area: 18,068 km^2
Length of coastline: 17,856 km
Population (1989): 3,053,300 (11.64% of total Canadian population)
Capital: Victoria
International airport: Vancouver

British Columbia is for many the most beautiful province in Canada. The visitor can head for the mountains, hills, forests or lakes – there is every kind of scenery you could wish for. This makes tourism a big money spinner for the province.

The fishing industry emphasises the use of modern, long-range fishing vessels that trawl the deep seas rather than the coastal fishing that has resulted in the quaint villages of the Atlantic Provinces.

There is little arable land in the province, and what there is is mostly given over to the growing of fodder for animals. There are rich mineral resources, however, and tremendous hydroelectric power and huge forests which fuel the forest industry.

There is a major fruit growing area in the interior of the province, known as the Okanagan Valley, while in the south near Osoyoos is the only desert in Canada.

The climate is mild, due to the warm westerly winds and the Pacific Ocean. Along the coast, it is often cool and wet. Winters are never severe, but mild and wet, and summers are warm. The interior is much drier and hotter in summer and colder in winter.

The province is Canada's window to the Pacific and Asia.

The capital of British Columbia is Victoria, on Vancouver Island. It is British Columbia's second largest city and sits on the south end of Vancouver Island: a genteel town with a distinctly British air.

Vancouver, which sits on the mainland just opposite, is the province's largest city and Canada's third largest. Picturesquely situated between mountains and sea, it is blessed with a very mild, though often wet, climate. There is a large and vibrant Chinatown which covers eight square blocks, and Cantonese can often be heard in the shopping areas.

One feature unique to British Columbia is the Adams River sockeye salmon run, when adult salmon struggle up the river to reach spawning grounds where they find a mate, spawn and die. This occurs every year around the month of October, and once every four years, a bumper run occurs when millions of salmon return in such abundant numbers that they turn the river a crimson colour. The last such run was in October 1990. The next one will be in 1994.

Northwest Territories

Total land area: 3,379,698 km^2
Total fresh water area: 133,294 km^2
Length of coastline: 111,249 km
Population (1989): 53,300 (0.2% of total Canadian population)
Capital: Yellowknife
International airport: None

The Northwest Territories occupy a vast area, more than one-third the area of the whole country. It is Canada's frontier land – the land of the fur trader, hunter/trapper, explorer/adventurer and missionary.

In 1789, Alexander Mackenzie, one of Canada's great explorers, travelled the length of the river that is now named after him. In his wake came traders, missionaries and prospectors. The area was monopolised by the Hudson's Bay Company, which had sole trading privileges in the territories for many years. When, in 1870, the Hudson's Bay Company sold its privileges, the area was opened to free traders. Gold discovered in Yellowknife Bay in the early 30s caused prospectors to flock to the area.

The western part of the Northwest Territories and the Mackenzie River valley are the best-known and most accessible parts. The capital is Yellowknife, which has a population of about 14,000. This represents almost a quarter of the total population of the region. Yellowknife is a modern city with high-rises, hotels, restaurants, a museum and two gold mines. The old part of the town is a picturesque collection of old gold rush buildings. Tourists use it as a base for trips to the more remote regions of the north. Access to Yellowknife by road is from Edmonton, 1600 kilometres along the Mackenzie Highway. Apart from this highway and its network of offshoot roads, the rest of the territories is accessible only by air.

Yukon

Total land area: 482,517 km^2
Total fresh water area: 4481 km^2
Length of coastline: 343 km
Population (1989): 25,300 (0.1% of total Canadian population)
Capital: Whitehorse
International airport: None

Yukon in Indian means 'greatest' – an apt name indeed for a land that is full of jagged mountains, boundless waterways, infinite wildlife and sharply contrasting seasons.

It has vast mineral wealth, and mining is the Yukon's major industry. However, most of its resources have yet to be unearthed because of the harsh climate and rugged terrain.

The Yukon is almost synonymous with gold, which was discovered in the area in the late 19th century. The discovery resulted in the world's last great gold rush. People flocked to the Klondike from all over the world. Dawson City became boom city, with a population of more than 30,000 people then. Today, only 1600 keep it alive.

Whitehorse was the stopping point en route to the Klondike, and when the gold turned to dust, it was also the stopping point for those who made it back. Today it is the administrative capital of the Yukon, and about 20,000 people live here.

Chapter Two

THIS LAND IS YOUR LAND

The history of Canada is one of immigration and the filling up of empty spaces. Much larger than their continental neighbour to the south, the lands that are now part of the sovereign nation of Canada have been the scene of constant challenges between one group and another for supremacy. Today Canada brings together 10 provinces and two territories, stretching from the Atlantic to the Pacific Ocean and from the 49th parallel to the frozen lands of the Arctic Circle. The people of the provinces and territories are united into one nation with a common identity and many similarities in its vision of itself. However, there are still differences and tensions within Canada. Both the similarities and the differences are the result of historical events which have shaped the country into what it has become today.

'THE PEOPLE'

The first two groups of people to come to North America in the earliest times were almost always referred to by later European arrivals as 'Indians' or 'Eskimos'. In neither case is this an accurate indicator of their origins nor even pleasing to themselves as a description of their people. In fact native Canadians prefer to refer to themselves in their own languages simply as 'the People' – the undisputed first inhabitants of the land.

It seems likely that the first group of the People to come to Canada crossed from somewhere in Asia by means of a now non-existent land bridge some time during the last Ice Age. Grouped in small wandering tribes, they roamed the ice-covered land in search of food. As much of the surface of Canada was still covered by glaciers and vast sheets of ice, game was not always easy to find. The animals that they managed to hunt and kill provided them with food, shelter, warmth and clothing, and for many centuries this way of life suited the People perfectly. However, as the ice began to recede and vegetation took its place, the nomadic hunting tribes began to gather some of the wild plants for food. When this happened, it was a short move from the gathering stage to the point at which agriculture itself started to develop. So some of the original tribal groups stopped wandering and began to cultivate the land deliberately. Maize – often called Indian corn – made its first appearance, and although the crops that the early cultivators farmed did not encourage anything like the stage of agricultural development that took place in Europe, gradually a stable and prosperous group of gathering communities began to emerge, scattered across the face of North America. There was very little, if any, communication between these groups due to the enormous distances involved. But the People had begun to stake their claims to the land – claims that would be hotly contested later. For the time being, however, the People's settlement process continued gradually and mostly peacefully over many centuries – until the beginning of exploration in North America by European navigators and the inevitable cultural conflicts that followed.

THE ARRIVAL OF THE EUROPEANS

It is still not known exactly who the first Europeans to come to North America were, but legends – and some recently recovered artifacts – suggest that the Norsemen of Scandinavia landed on the east coast of North America (including Newfoundland) long before the arrival of Christopher Columbus in the New World. Probably other European fishermen also discovered the New World before Columbus – the Grand Banks off the coast of Newfoundland were known for centuries as one of the most prolific fishing grounds in the world, and there may have been permanent fishing communities in the parts of Canada adjacent to them, such as Newfoundland, as early as the 13th century. However, it was not until the early European colonisers came that the native people received the first significant challenge to their way of life. The French were the first to realise the enormous potential of this vast undeveloped land and particularly the abundance of natural resources which it possessed – in fact the same kinds of resources that the native communities had been relying on for centuries. French explorers (and later English ones too) were initially looking for furs, much in demand for the European fashion styles of the day, thus fetching a high price in the markets of Europe. As a result, men such as Samuel de Champlain and Pierre de la Verendrye became the first Europeans to penetrate the interior of Canada, and through their travels, spearheaded the first contacts between the original peoples and the European settlers who soon followed and began to take possession of the land for themselves.

At first the native peoples with whom these early adventurers came in contact were more than eager to sell to the newcomers all the fur they wanted for the new wonders they could get in exchange:

knives, copper pots, clothing – and guns. But relying on the native people to satisfy the supply could not last long. The British weren't far behind in the race to exploit this new country either – the Company of Gentlemen Adventurers into Hudson Bay (now known simply as the Hudson's Bay Company) was created in 1660 under the auspices of the British King Charles II, and the rivalry between the English and the French, which has coloured much of the development of this new land, began in earnest.

Struggle for Supremacy

Settlement almost always follows trade and so the next 100 years had a profound impact on the way of life that had been carried on uninterrupted by the native peoples over the preceding centuries. In one way or another the next period was one of almost continuous wars between the English and the French over rights to both trade and settlement. The Hudson's Bay Company staked its claim to all the land which fell into the watershed of Hudson's Bay, where it had first established trading posts, while the French, using their system of *coureurs de bois,* had penetrated with their large canoes further and further into the mainland surrounding and leading away from the St Lawrence River. Of course no attention was paid to the rights of the native people and any interference from them usually resulted in either attempts to convert them to the European way of thinking (often accompanied by religious conversion) or outright extermination. As a result of this invasion, by the early 1700s French settlement was well established, particularly along the shores of the St Lawrence River, while the British had extended northwards from their southern colonies and established strings of trading posts close to, or even on, the territory claimed by the French. The rivalry between British and French finally came to a head in 1759 when the French forces under the command of General Montcalm were besieged by the English troops of General James Wolfe in an attempt to capture the French stronghold of Quebec. The British success in this battle became one

A re-enactment of a famous battle in an Ontario park.

of the pivotal points in the course of Canadian history by entrenching British supremacy over those areas of Canada which were later to become Quebec and Ontario, and by laying the foundation for the resentment and distrust which persists into modern Canadian life.

Spread of British Culture

The British domination of settlement and trade in North America was not to go unchallenged, however – and not only by the French. In 1776, Britain's own American colonies rebelled against their colonial masters in the American War of Independence. As a result, some of the British immigrants began to move northwards to stake their claims to new land in Canada which was still firmly within the jurisdiction of Britain and so removed from the influence of the rebellious American colonists. These Loyalists, as they became known, settled mainly along the shores of northern Lake Ontario and in the Maritime Provinces, establishing a formal British presence. They brought with them a culture which was very different from both that of the natives and the French culture which was still flourishing not many miles away up the St Lawrence.

It did not take long for these new British settlers to have an impact on the way Canada was governed, and to tip the balance even further away from the previous domination of the fledgling economy by the fur trading interests located in Quebec and Montreal.

THE CREATION OF CANADA

In 1791, the old Province of Quebec, created after the fall of New France to the British in 1763, was divided into two parts: Lower and Upper Canada. Lower Canada, with Quebec City as its centre, remained mainly French in character in spite of the fact that it was now under British rule, while Upper Canada was controlled by the British elements who had settled in the area after the American War of Independence. The capital city of York (now Toronto) was very much influenced by these staunchly British Loyalist settlers.

However, the antagonism between the remaining British colonies in North America and the newly independent country to the south did not subside. Much of the conflict centred around the insistence of the British to retain control over shipping in the St Lawrence River and the Great Lakes. This meant – in the British opinion – that they had the right to stop and search American ships to see if they were carrying aid to France, with whom the British were once again at war. The Americans finally declared war on Britain and its colonies in 1812. There were several land skirmishes during the two years that this war lasted. Several naval battles were also fought on Lake Ontario, but in the end neither side gained a strategic advantage over the other and the War of 1812 – the only occasion when Canada and the United States have come into actual armed conflict – was eventually terminated by the Treaty of Ghent in 1814. The issues that had led to its outbreak were finally settled three years later in the Rush-Bagot agreement between Britain and the United States.

Following the resolution of the War of 1812 there was considerable growth in population in both Canadas with the result that a sense of nationalism began to emerge for the first time. The governors of both provinces, appointed by the British king, began to feel and see challenges to their formerly undisputed authority, some of them resulting in outright political rebellion. Lord Durham, sent out by the British to investigate the cause of the political unrest, suggested in his report of 1839 that the two provinces be united once again (partly to facilitate the total assimilation of the French Canadians) and that this new single entity be given its own legislature with considerably increased political powers. The British government agreed and this union took place in 1841, creating the new Province of Canada.

During this period, the maritime provinces close to the Atlantic had also been growing in population and were establishing their own identities. New Brunswick, Nova Scotia and Prince Edward Island, as well as Newfoundland, had attracted their share of settlers from both the French and British communities. Although all these areas had a certain degree of autonomy, they were still under the direct control of the British government in London, as was the Province of Canada. During the 1840s and 1850s all the new provinces began to face problems brought about by a rapidly industrialising world. To cope with these problems and to help spread the load, talks began among the leaders of the various areas on the possibility of union. In 1867 the provinces of Canada, Prince Edward Island, Nova Scotia and New Brunswick joined together under the British North America Act into one country. This Confederation, as it was called, was only a limited beginning to the creation of what we now know as the country of Canada, but it did set the stage for Canada to become more than a reflection of the cultures and beliefs of France and England.

THE MAKING OF MODERN CANADA

Confederation brought together two peoples very different in culture and outlook who had reached a political agreement purely for economic reasons. It was an uneasy partnership as the history and culture

37

of the British and French pulled them in such different directions. Canada had become, in effect, a bi-cultural country, but not yet a multi-cultural one.

Up to and following Confederation, the native population had been steadily pushed westwards by the increasing British and French settlement in the east. The rock masses of the Canadian Shield had now become the great physical and psychological dividing line – to the east there were civilisation and sophistication, while to the west were the empty lands of Indians and buffaloes all the way to other British settlements along the Pacific shore in British Columbia. As a result, there was considerable concern among some Canadians that these empty lands would soon be swallowed up by the ever-expanding United States if steps were not taken to populate them with Canadians. The British-controlled Hudson's Bay Company still owned much of this empty land and so arrangements were made by the Canadian government to purchase it from them, leading quickly to the establishment in 1870 of the first Canadian political unit west of the Canadian Shield – the Province of Manitoba. Following this, British Columbia agreed to join in the Confederation in 1871, following a promise that a railway line would be built, linking coast to coast. After some political tribulations, this line was indeed completed and the last spike hammered in at Craigellachie, high in the Rockies, in 1885.

Colonisation of Empty Lands

At last the vast empty lands that stretched for miles between Manitoba and British Columbia had become accessible from the east and so could be populated. Thus a concentrated effort was made to attract new settlers from outside the country to fill this new – but still very desolate – land. Through a massive publicity campaign, promising free farm land to those who came to Canada and successfully established themselves there, new immigrants were attracted from all over Europe to Canada. They were taken westwards on special trains run along the newly completed Canadian Pacific transcontinental

A historic pioneer village. Here young schoolgirls have their hands inspected before entering the classroom.

line. Some of these new settlers were experienced farmers who had never had the good fortune to own their own land and who were overjoyed to accept and develop the tracts of virgin land that were given to them by the Canadian government. Others were new both to the country and to the type of backbreaking labour they had volunteered for. Although some of the newcomers gave up and went home, the descendants of many of the original settlers still farm the same prairie land today, though on a scale and in a style that must have been unimaginable to their hard-working ancestors who had to develop the land with basic farming implements and their own bare hands.

Eventually, this vast influx of new settlers resulted in the formation of the new provinces of Saskatchewan and Alberta in 1905. With the exception of Newfoundland, which after many years of deliberation finally joined the Canadian Confederation in 1949, the physical

39

structure of Canada as we now know it was essentially in place.

As Canada grew and prospered, individual communities both contributed to and benefited from this prosperity. The first three decades of this century were a time of great growth for Canadians, and even though the simmering dispute between English and French flared up again briefly over the issue of conscription into the British army during World War I, on the surface Canada appeared to be becoming an extremely prosperous and successful multi-cultural experiment. However, this sense of pride and harmony began to crumble when the Great Depression of the 1930s hit Canada hard. New protest movements were formed, especially in Quebec and the farming communities of the west, leading to the development of new left-wing political parties, such as Social Credit. This popular unrest, although briefly halted by Canada's involvement in World War II, drew attention to the fact that some of the original underlying tensions between the peoples and regions of the country had never been completely dealt with or satisfactorily solved.

Conflict and Resolution

After the externally imposed tension of World War II, which had temporarily diverted attention away from the internal problems of Canada, had receded, a number of independence movements surfaced during the 1950s and 1960s, a definite sign of the growing feeling of disunity among the very different ethnic populations. The 'Quiet Revolution' in Quebec was an attempt by the Quebec and federal governments to work together to pay more attention to the specific problems of the French Canadians in Quebec, by methods such as the establishment of the Bi-lingualism and Bi-culturalism Commission in 1965. Prime ministers John Diefenbaker and Lester Pearson also tried to give Canada as a whole a greater sense of unity by the adoption of the Maple Leaf flag and the holding of Expo '67 in Montreal on the country's 100th birthday. However, these efforts did not go without opposition, as embodied by the FLQ (Front de Libération de Quebec),

The maple leaf is today a symbol of Canada. Its adoption as the national flag gave Canadians a greater sense of unity.

a home-grown terrorist organisation. Prime Minister Pierre Eliot Trudeau, a French Canadian himself and an extremely popular choice as national leader at the time of his election, may be best remembered for his tough stand against Quebec separatist terrorism during the early 1970s. But he is probably more well known for being the prime minister who finally won Canada's own written constitution, with the right to amend and change it without resort to the British Parliament as had formerly been the case.

However, in spite of all the federal efforts to define the best possible relationship between Quebec and the rest of the country, political unrest in Quebec culminated in the election of the Parti Quebecois in 1976 on a separatist platform of sovereignty association with Canada (which would grant political but not economic independence from the rest of the country). In the event, a referendum in 1979 rejected any form of outright separation, but did little to reconcile French Canadians with their English neighbours.

Unrest also resurfaced in the western provinces of the country, which had long felt neglected by the concentration of political and economic power in eastern Canada. The need for change in the region began to be emphasised, even leading to talk of the formation of a western-based Reform Party if the problems of western Canadians were not soon addressed satisfactorily by the government in Ottawa.

During the 70s and 80s native Canadians too began to demonstrate dissatisfaction with their lot and with the land sacrifices that their ancestors had been called upon to make. Some of the earliest treaty arrangements had been negotiated with individual bands and were little more than licences for outright exploitation of their lands and resources. Legislation during the 20th century had begun to redress this imbalance by providing special privileges, such as tax relief, for registered native Canadians, but most of the native population were still encouraged by law to live on their own reserves and not to mix with their non-native neighbours. As a result, political agitation among the various native groups centred around these three issues: to have the aboriginal peoples of Canada recognised as a 'distinct society' – a phrase first used by the French Canadians to describe themselves – to include special provisions in any constitutional legislation to define clearly their place in Canadian society and to settle, once and for all, native claims for land and legal rights.

To counter all these feelings of alienation, the federal government continued its efforts in trying to bring a sense of unity to Canada, especially with the repatriation of the Canadian Constitution in 1982 and other specific regional legislative attempts to heal the rifts that seemed to be developing in all areas of the country.

CANADA IN THE 90s

Although the tensions that exist beneath the surface are real and in need of solution, Canada in the 1990s is still more than just the sum of its parts. However much economic, social and linguistic issues threaten to disunite the country – more profoundly now than they have ever done since Confederation – there is still a desire among most Canadians to make their country work and to resist its disintegration and subsequent inevitable absorption by the United States.

To achieve this, both the federal and the Quebec governments began initiatives in 1990 to find out what needs to be done to reunite the country in a meaningful way. In spite of growing regional anti-French and anti-English sentiments, these commissions represent a serious attempt to prevent further disunity. The issue of aboriginal rights and land claims is also being actively examined by the federal government, through a series of high level meetings and Royal Commissions, in an attempt to reach an agreement on the rightful status of the native Canadians in their homeland.

The need for action on these divisive issues is becoming clearer as Canada advances into the 1990s and its attitudes about itself and its citizens undergo a fundamental change. What is needed – and what the current government commissions are seeking – is the promotion of a common vision of what unites all Canadians and makes them contribute equally to the success of the country. Finding this will not be easy, especially given the historical legacy of Canada, and it will require compromise and sacrifice. But if it can be achieved, Canada will emerge by the end of the 20th century as a strong and united country, having renewed its basic traits of tolerance and understanding, and having found peaceful solutions to its problems of division.

Chapter Three

THE CANADIAN VISION

Probably because Canada's history has been so full of cultural conflict and confusion, there has been interminable discussion among Canadians in an attempt to define what a Canadian really is and what vision of the world he espouses. The debate continues to this day, so narrowing down the nature of Canada and its view of itself is nearly impossible. All that anyone can really do is to examine what has been said, written and implied about the nature of this country, but any final understanding must always be the responsibility of the individual to reach by drawing conclusions from both the concrete and abstract clues that Canada and its citizens provide from their daily lives.

John Porter, a Canadian social historian, in a well-known book about Canada published in the 1960s, referred to Canada as a 'vertical mosaic' in which different ethnic groups and social classes lived in a clearly defined relationship to one another. It is this concept of the 'mosaic' rather than the more American concept of the 'melting pot' which has had the major influence on what Canada has become today. The difference between 'melting pot' and 'mosaic' lies in the way in which a country and its inhabitants integrate new arrivals into the social fabric of the country. In Canadian terms, what the mosaic concept has really meant is that newcomers to Canada – and nearly all Canadians are either newcomers themselves or have fairly recent ancestors who were new arrivals – have been encouraged both to retain their own cultural identity and to attempt to become part of some overall Canadian identity at the same time. This has never been an easy task as it has really meant trying to do two things at the same time, one of which was very ill-defined, and it has led to considerable discussion and confusion within Canada itself as to whether the Canadian identity itself is different from or the same as the sum of all the various cultural parts which have been contributed to it.

Thus anyone who lives in Canada for any length of time will be confronted by the two questions that Canadians are continually asking themselves: what does being Canadian mean and how should I view myself in terms of my own Canadian identity?

WHAT IS A CANADIAN?

Pierre Berton, one of Canada's best known authors and historians, writes in his book *Why We Act Like Canadians* that Canadians have come to terms with the tensions that obsess them, slowly and cautiously in the Canadian fashion, and that they are beginning to understand that these tensions will not go away; so they must learn to live with them, adapt to them and survive them, just as they have survived their appalling geography.

In talking of the Canadian obsession with tension, Berton may have put his finger on something fundamental to understanding how most Canadians think of themselves. Dealing with tension does lead to caution and most Canadians will agree that they are a cautious people. Certainly Canadians lack the flamboyance of the Americans who insist on 'liberty at any price', and as Berton claims, seem to prefer the concept of a democracy which 'is dispensed from the heavens like gentle rain' rather than the American kind which 'sprouts upwards from the grass'.

Canadian cautiousness comes perhaps mainly from the fact that the Canadian people have always been caught between the demands of two cultures, and also between the paternalism of Britain and France on the one hand and the aggressive egalitarianism of the United States on the other. Many people – both inside and outside the country – see Canada as a compromise between the two, without either the reserve of the British or the brashness of the Americans, and this seems to be borne out in the attitude that Canadians try to project of themselves to others. But in trying to incorporate the best of two worlds into one national identity, some of their original strengths may have become diluted. As a result, many Canadians still say that there is no truly Canadian vision per se – though most Canadian writers, poets and dramatists would tell you differently – and that what Canadians are in effect is simply a pale reflection of some vast cultural and sociological mix. However, this ignores the fact that the perceived identity of the country as a peculiarly successful blend of understanding and acceptance is a vision shared by many Canadians, and that this could only have been achieved through the unique set of circumstances which has shaped the special nature of the Canadian people as a whole.

Statistics tell some of the story that makes Canadians a special people. Out of a Canadian population of around 27 million, some 10 million now live in big metropolitan areas like Toronto, Montreal and Vancouver, and have adopted the outlook of big city dwellers, while 2 million people still live in a completely rural – and predominantly

Although Canadians are a conservative people, traditional blacksmiths like this one can only be seen in a special historical village.

traditional – lifestyle on the farms that dot the countryside. However, this represents a significant population shift in such a comparatively young country, as up to World War II, 25 to 30% of Canadians lived away from the cities and on farms. Today these farms are fast disappearing, changing the face of the country – and its attitudes – in the process. The remainder of the population lives in the smaller towns and cities spread across the country, reflecting both the traditional values of a rural society and the more progressive attitudes of the urbanite. This mix of traditional and progressive attitudes is peculiarly Canadian and accounts in no small measure for both some of the special ways in which Canada sees the world and also for its internal divisions.

Thus, although Canada today is predominantly an urban, mobile

47

society with a progressive contemporary vision, it is still tempered by the fact that many city dwellers are newcomers to city life, either recently transplanted from smaller Canadian communities or from completely different communities in other countries who have come to Canada seeking a new life and a new vision for themselves. For this reason alone, any static definition of what a Canadian is is extremely hard to achieve, and will continue to be as long as the sociological mix of Canadians is constantly changing through internal population shifts and constant immigration from a variety of foreign cultures.

CANADIAN STEREOTYPES

Although an actual definition of a true Canadian might be hard to reach, there is no shortage of Canadian stereotypes, most of them unflattering. In the 1980s the Canadian comedy team of Bob and Doug Mackenzie specialised in portraying the stereotypical Canadian as a boozing outdoorsman whose ignorance of the world around him was only exceeded by his own stupidity. Bob and Doug's stereotypes were limited in their vocabulary and their conversation – liberally sprinkled with the addition of 'eh', a supposed Canadianism – revolved round fishing and the price of beer. Most Canadians found the observations of Bob and Doug Mackenzie funny, but also a little disturbing as there was no doubt a grain of truth in the picture.

In 1952, noted Canadian actor Don Harron created the character of Charlie Farquharson, a rustic who has since become one of Canada's most endearing – and enduring – comic stereotypes. Charlie is an uneducated man with an interesting vocabulary and strong opinions about his country, its history and the way it is run. As Charlie Farquharson, Don Harron has often appeared on television and radio to comment on Canadian society and to encourage it to look at itself in a humorous way. Charlie Farquharson's comments have also been collected into a series of books – the most famous of which is *Charlie Farquharson's Histry of Canada* – which have found their way onto most Canadian bookshelves.

But if you ask many Canadians today to describe the way in which Canadians are stereotyped, both by themselves and by outsiders – especially by Americans – you will get comments about Canadians being seen as a fundamentally boring people, living in a land of perpetual ice and snow, and surrounded by polar bears and men in red coats. Most Canadian stereotypes are rarely positive and seem to emphasise either only the scenic beauty of the country or the backwardness and conservatism of the people. To be fair, however, in a more positive light, Canada and Canadians have also achieved an international reputation as constructive compromisers, especially negotiators and peacemakers, capable of seeing all sides of a position.

Here are some comments on Canadians made by a cross-section of current observers of Canada:

'Historically, a Canadian is an American who rejects the revolution.'
– Northrop Frye, literary philosopher

'I think our identity will have to be something which is partly British, partly French, partly American, partly derived from a variety of other influences which are too numerous even to catalogue.'
– Eugene Forsey, government senator

'Dull and introverted and all the rest of it though we may be, Canadians have as a people a national gift for tolerance and an acquired skill at compromise.'
– Richard Gwyn, newspaper columnist

'Years ago, the British critic Ron Bryden said to me, "Canadians are nice, very nice and they expect everybody else to be very nice"; and I have yet to come up with a better definition.'
– Mordecai Richler, novelist

'The problem is that Canada is not so much a nation, more an act of faith … I asked dozens of people what made them specifically

Canadian and every single one defined their country purely in terms of not being American.'

– Simon Hoggart, journalist

'A Canadian is somebody who knows how to make love in a canoe.'
– Pierre Berton, media personality

'Sociologically I am an American. Psychologically, a Canadian, Sentimentally, a Quebecois… Everywhere I see dualities.'

– Clark Blaise, author

'Well it's a good place to live. But that's all Canada is – just a good place to live. Canadians have lost their destiny.'

– Donald Creighton, historian

'Perhaps then, Canada is not so much a country as magnificent raw material for a country: and perhaps the question is not "Who are we?" but "What are we going to make of ourselves?"'

– Alden Nowlan, poet

MULTI-CULTURALISM IN CANADA

Just as there are many views of what a Canadian is, there are also many myths about the nature of Canada's multi-culturalism. The most enduring is that Canada is not really a multi-cultural country, but a creation of the British to which all other cultures have become subservient. Up to the end of the last century there might have been some truth in this as there can be no doubt that the British government did try to create Canada in its own image – especially at the expense of the French. But ever since the arrival of the large waves of immigrants from Europe before World War I and after World War II, Canada's character has changed and its population base includes people whose origins are as diverse as the world itself. In the 1980s alone, more than 1 million immigrants came to Canada from more

The Mennonites were among the first Europeans to come to Canada.

than 100 different countries, settling in cities and small towns, and changing their character for ever. Surprisingly perhaps, this influx of ethnically diverse newcomers into what were predominantly enclaves of western culture does not seem to have led to any kind of overt racism, as it has done in some areas of the United States. Canada and Canadians have a remarkable record for tolerance and this characteristic seems to ease the absorption of newcomers. As a result there is little evidence of racial conflict in the country, even in its major cities.

In fact, the ever-growing multi-cultural nature of the country is now reflected in the attention that is paid to it by both private and public agencies. The federal government Department of State as well as the provincial Departments of Citizenship and Social Services have a number of services and publications designed specifically to assist newcomers to Canada. The right to an interpreter in a court of law is now enshrined in the Canadian Charter of Rights and Freedoms, while many educational authorities are introducing both extensive

English as a Second Language and Heritage Language programmes in the schools. The concept of the vertical mosaic with the Anglo-Saxon cultures at the top is now thankfully a dying one and does not seem to be replaced by any other kind of national stereotype.

The mosaic is still growing and increasing in complexity, with the result that by the year 2000, there will be more Canadians with origins outside North America than there will be from within. This fact alone will change the nature of the country and its needs forever. Acceptance, understanding and tolerance of many cultures has become part of the Canadian way of life and those who come to this country in the future will find that these Canadian traditions are alive and well. However, the Canadian stereotype may well undergo some change over the years while – probably – Canada's seemingly unending search for its true identity will still go on.

THE POLITICAL SPECTRUM

Canadian politics obviously play a very important part in defining what Canada is now and what it will become in the next century. The Canadian democratic traditions are very open, and Canadians have strong opinions about their politicians and their multi-level system of government, federal (national), provincial and municipal.

Canada is a member of the Commonwealth of Nations and a constitutional monarchy. As such, it is headed by a Governor General, who acts as the representative of Queen Elizabeth II in Canada and exercises the monarch's functions on her behalf. The Governor General is appointed by the Queen on the recommendation of the prime minister of Canada, and usually stays in office for five years. He is granted the use of his own personal standard which flies over his two official residences: Rideau Hall in Ottawa and the Governor's Wing in the Quebec Citadel. Some of his functions are the summoning and dissolution of Parliament, the appointment of ambassadors and the commissioning of officers in the Armed Forces. He also gives royal assent to any new law passed by the House of Commons and is consulted in the same way that the Queen would be if she lived in Canada. The first Canadian to hold the post was Vincent Massey who was appointed in 1952, and the first woman Governor General was Jeanne Sauve, who was appointed in 1983. The current Governor General is The Right Honourable Ray Hnatyshn, appointed in 1989.

The headquarters of the federal government have moved location many times, but since Confederation, they have been in Ottawa, formerly Bytown, at the head of the Rideau Canal. The Canadian Parliament is divided into two houses, the House of Commons and the Senate. The former comprises elected representatives and the latter appointees for life by the prime minister. All new bills require the support of both houses and the assent of the Governor General before becoming laws. The federal parliament is responsible for matters that affect the country as a whole: national defence, citizenship, foreign policy, economic policy and currency.

Provincial parliaments are located in all the capital cities of the 10 Canadian provinces, and are responsible under the constitution for the administration of all provincial matters: highways, social services, education, health care, industrial growth and the environment. The two territories have their own administrative councils for the same purposes, but, due to their much smaller populations, these do not have the same degree of autonomy as the provincial parliaments.

Local government is headquartered in small towns and cities all over the country, and looks after schools, libraries, public utilities, parks and recreation facilities and urban planning.

Political Parties

There are three major political parties in Canada, all of which are represented at the provincial and federal levels. At the time of writing (1991) the Conservative (or Tory) Party is in power federally, led by Prime Minister Brian Mulroney, and represents the right wing of the political spectrum – belief in private enterprise and the rights of the individual over the group. The Liberal Party, the official opposition led by Jean Chrétien, represents the middle of the road philosophy, and tries to steer a course between the Tories and the New Democratic Party, led by Audrey MacLachlan, which is more leftist in ideology, but like many things Canadian, is not too far from the centre.

In addition to the three major parties, there are two smaller splinter parties at the federal level – the Bloc Quebecois, which advocates the separation of Quebec from the rest of Canada, and the Reform Party, a western-Canada-based group which wants to see a major reform of the political structure in Canada and more responsibility returned to the individual voter.

At the provincial level, there are a number of other significant political groups, again predominantly in Quebec and the west of the country. Quebec has an official opposition in the Parti Quebecois, a separatist party, which has once already tried – and failed – to bring about the separation of Quebec, and which would like to be in a position to try again. The Social Credit Party in the west has a considerable number of political supporters who are hostile to the federal government's policies.

The municipal governments, which control all local activities, are not as politically oriented as their federal or provincial counterparts. They are also more directly responsive to those they represent because of their proximity. But they are still subject to persuasion from the political parties on issues that involve funding from higher levels of government.

Regrettably, however, there is a strong cynicism among the Canadian population at the moment about all political processes and the politicians who control them. Politics in Canada is not regarded as a noble profession but more of a self-serving one. It will take strong commitment from aspiring politicians in the future to overcome this and restore trust among the electorate that the government and its policies really operate in the best interests of the citizens of the country as a whole.

THE CANADIAN CHARTER OF RIGHTS AND FREEDOMS

On April 17, 1982, Canada gained for the first time a written constitution, which among other things, gave certain legal guarantees to all Canadians. This Charter of Rights and Freedoms includes four fundamental freedoms – of conscience and religion, of thought, belief, opinion and expression, of peaceful assembly, and of association – and a number of other rights associated with these. These rights include the right to life, liberty and security of the person, the right to perform certain actions if suspected of a crime and to be presumed innocent until proven guilty, and rights guaranteeing equality under the law, regardless of race, national or ethnic origin, colour, religion, sex, age and mental or physical ability. Each of these areas is clearly defined in the Charter of Rights and in any provincial legislation dealing with these areas, and any violation can be challenged in court. Most provinces also retain an ombudsman who investigates alleged breaches of civil rights and rectifies any miscarriages of justice.

Canadians take the rights and freedoms granted to them very seriously – more seriously perhaps than any other legal aspect of their lives – and there is always great pressure from the community when it is felt that one of these rights is being infringed upon. Laws relating to contentious social issues, such as abortion, have frequently been the subject of challenges, and in spite of sometimes strongly-held conflicting prejudices, the rights of the individual are usually upheld and safeguarded. This gives rise to controversy and occasionally social unrest, but one thing most Canadians do accept is the fairness of the concept that an individual has the right to make his own decisions in situations which do not affect others.

These constitutional rights override and nullify any federal or provincial law which conflicts with them – subject to a successful court challenge – and cannot be repealed or amended by any parliament or legislature. The only possible exception to the operation of the Charter of Rights and Freedoms is its provision for the federal parliament or a province to declare that one of its own laws shall operate within its jurisdiction in spite of an obvious conflict with one of the stated rights and freedoms. This provision for 'opting out' is valid for five years but can be renewed for a further five-year period.

Chapter Four

IN THE SHADOW OF BIG BROTHER

- John F. Kennedy on Canada: 'Geography made us neighbours. History made us friends. And economics made us partners.'
- Ronald Reagan: 'No other country in the world is more important to the United States than Canada, and we are blessed to have such a nation on our northern border.'
- Pierre Trudeau said sharing a border with the United States is like 'sleeping with an elephant. No matter how friendly or even-tempered is the beast, if I may call it that, one is affected by every twitch and grunt!'
- Brian Mulroney: '… we get less attention down there than Cuba,

Nicaragua, El Salvador, you name it. To get a mention down in Washington, you have to be either Wayne Gretzky or a good snowstorm.'

– some observations by US and Canadian politicians on the ties that bind the two countries

THE INVISIBLE FRONTIER

The 49th Parallel that divides the North American continent into Canada in the north and the United States in the south has been called the world's longest undefended boundary between two nations. It is 6379 kilometres long.

Just how invisible is that border? It was invisible during the American Revolution (1775–1783) when about 50,000 Loyalist settlers left America because of their loyalty to Britain. They settled mainly in the Atlantic Provinces and in Ontario.

It was invisible during America's involvement in the Vietnam War, when many anti-war protesters and objectors of conscience copied their 18th century forebears and fled north to escape being drafted into the army.

It is still almost invisible today as many daily border crossings are made with the least amount of formality, and news, information and ideas flow across with ease.

There are 26 million Canadians versus 250 million Americans south of the border. This difference in size and the proximity of the two nations often results in the Canadian nation feeling rather overwhelmed by its bigger and stronger 'cousin' in the south. Every day, Canadians are exposed to the American media, whose influence is hard to escape. Books and magazines, movies and radio and television bring American thoughts, ideas, issues and products into Canadian homes. Many American publications and news weeklies like *Time* and *Newsweek* fill the magazine racks of Canadian stores, whereas many Americans, on the other hand, have not even heard of, much less read, *Macleans*, Canada's equivalent news magazine.

The American influence is even more pervasive on television – Canadians can tune in to many American TV stations linked to networks like CBS, NBC, ABC and PBS (Public Broadcasting Service) as easily as CBC (Canadian Broadcasting Corporation). Some people may not even know whether they are watching an American or Canadian production. Even Canadian news programmes contain so much more about American events than American newscasts do about Canada.

Cross-Border Trips

If you are Canadian, you can drive across the border with the greatest of ease. A brief and polite enquiry from a friendly customs officer regarding how long you expect to be down south is about the only formality you might encounter. If you are a newly-landed immigrant or permanent resident, there will be a quick glance at your passport just to make sure that all is in order.

Canadians who live near the border often go across to do their shopping. 'I often cross the line to Bellingham (a US border town just half an hour from Vancouver) to get my groceries and fill the tank,' says a Vancouverite. Petrol (or gas, as it is called in North America) and many other items are cheaper in the United States. A consumer report in a British Columbia newspaper made comparisons between identical items sold in a big store in the United States and its sister store in Canada and concluded that there were many reasons why Canadians love to go shopping across the line: many of the American items were a good 50% cheaper, even after taking into account the conversion value of the US and Canadian dollars, customs duties, provincial sales tax and the Goods and Services Tax (GST).

Since the introduction of the GST in January 1991, cross-border shopping is an issue that has assumed major proportions, with retailers in Canadian border towns complaining that they are losing business to the extent of going bankrupt. According to Statistics Canada, the federal body responsible for regularly gathering information about the country, the number of day trips by car into the United States during the first two months of 1991 increased by 21% over the same period in 1990. In February alone, almost 4 million Canadians made day-trips to the United States. There are traffic jams of more than two hours during weekends at the border crossings, so much so that Revenue Canada is experimenting with an express lane to speed things up – for a C$10 fee, a motorist will be allowed to use a special reserved lane. Instead of having to wait in line at customs, he is asked to indicate the value of goods he has bought in the States on a computer card, and duties and taxes will be charged to his credit card.

The Canada-US Free Trade Agreement

There are customs duties to be paid on purchases made in the United States, although much has been reduced or even eliminated because of the Canada-US Free Trade Agreement (FTA) which took effect on January 1, 1989. Under the agreement, duties on goods of US or Canadian origin that you buy for your own use will be progressively phased out according to a set timetable. Some common consumer goods which became free of duty immediately include calculators, computers, new motorcycles, skates, skis and word processing machines. Other items such as furniture, small appliances, leather suitcases and handbags, video games and paper products will become duty free over a period of five years. And items such as clothing, bed linen and bath towels, tobacco and large appliances will be duty free after 10 years.

Calling America!

The US-Canada border can be crossed just as easily by phone. One recent immigrant to Canada said she received an early lesson in this when she attempted to call San Francisco. Presuming that the international dialling code should be prefixed to the telephone number, she made her call, and was surprised when a voice answered, 'Nein, this is no San Francisco. Nein!' When the phone bill arrived, she discovered she had made a connection across the Atlantic to Switzerland!

So it is useful to remember that a phone call to the United States is just a 'non-local' call out of your area, for which you prefix a '1' to the number you want and the correct area code, just as you would for reaching any other part of Canada.

And the same goes for calling some places in the Caribbean – Bahamas, Barbados, Bermuda Islands, British Virgin Islands, Dominica, Jamaica, Puerto Rico and Trinidad!

THROUGH THE LOOKING GLASS

Outsiders may have trouble differentiating an American from a Canadian, but the North Americans themselves don't. As a friend once said, when he goes fishing and there is an American and a Canadian fishing near him, he knows which one is the American. Pressed for greater detail, he would not say more than, 'You can tell!'

The View from the South

Both Canadians and Americans wear jeans, T-shirts with the latest slogan, rock group or cartoon character on them, baseball caps and jogging shoes. They lead similar lifestyles.

Americans think of Canadians as being very much like them. When they go north, they see a lot of similarities with their own country. There is the mix of people from different cultures, dressed in similar way, the jeans and T-shirt wearing crowd, a similar urban sprawl in the cities and towns, bumper stickers with roughly the same messages, fast food restaurants. They find people who speak the same language (except in French Canada).

If they notice differences, it is probably in the way Canadians speak and spell, and other minor things. For instance, many Canadians say 'lef-tenant' rather than 'lieu-tenant' and 'schedule' with a soft 'c' rather than with a 'ske' sound. Canadians sign 'cheques' and not 'checks', pump their gas (petrol) in litres and not gallons, and seem to keep their streets so much cleaner.

The View from the North

Canadians, on the other hand, tend to emphasise the differences they see between themselves and Americans.

If you ask a Canadian what was the difference between himself and an American, he might say it was the American clenched-fist-to-the-chest kind of patriotism that Canadians don't exhibit. Canadian thinker and literary critic Northrop Frye said that 'American students have been conditioned from infancy to think of themselves as citizens of one of the world's great powers. Canadians are conditioned from infancy to think of themselves as citizens of a country of uncertain identity, a confusing past and a hazardous future.'

The Canadian self-image is that of a reserved and modest person, not a back-slapping, familiar as can be, first-names-at-first-sight type. He associates violence with American society, a place where hand-

The peculiar Canadian sense of humour at work.

guns are a common possession. The Canadian may holiday in the States, but he is glad to come home where he feels safer, where the chances of being shot or mugged are less. And there are statistics to support this – according to *Gun Control,* edited by Robert Emmet Long, 'In one year during the 1980s, Great Britain had four handgun deaths, and Canada six, while the US had approximately 10,000.'

Canadians think Americans consider them boring! Americans generally know very little about their large neighbour in the north and it is an accepted Canadian opinion that they are not interested in learning more. When the American media suddenly pay attention to happenings in the north, as they did during the Meech Lake constitutional controversy, that is news. As a correspondent for the Canadian press put it: 'Editorial cartoonists are even paying attention. One in the San Francisco *Chronicle* showed President George and Barbara Bush reading in bed, trying to ignore a noisy fight in the next room: "That nice Canadian couple is at it again," says Barbara.'

Canadians seem used to the idea that Americans don't know very much about them or their country, and they accept it with some humour.

While many Canadians really dislike being mistaken for Americans, some seem to suffer from an identity crisis brought about by the close proximity of the two countries. In western Canada especially, some see a greater similarity between themselves and the United States than with Quebec and the eastern part of the country. There is resentment at being 'ruled over' by 'masters' in Ottawa; they see the promotion of French-English bilingualism as irrelevant, and promote the doctrine of separatism and the formation of an independent nation of Western Canada. For some, a political union with America in the south seems a more practical one.

For a more individual and personal look at US-Canadian relations, here are two interviews, with an American couple working and living in Canada, and with a Canadian in America. They speak of their experiences in living across the border:

Americans in Canada

Jim and Joanne came to Canada from the United States in 1984, when Jim's company transferred him to its Canadian branch. Their views of Canada and Canadians:

'Like most Americans, we had always been taught that the average Canadian's behaviour differed from that of the American. In some ways, we did find the attitudes and outlook in Canada to be what we expected. For example, I (Joanne) met and hugged an old friend during a casual encounter at a shopping mall in the friendly and uninhibited way with which most Americans would be socially quite comfortable, but which was not welcomed with the same degree of comfort by my Canadian friend!

'Although a natural reserve certainly is one of the characteristics that Americans notice about their northern neighbours, so again is loyalty. Canadians are very community oriented, and not only to their immediate social circle, but also in their jobs and in all situations in which membership of a specific group is important. One of the predominant differences between Americans and Canadians is that, while Americans pride themselves on and rejoice in being individuals per se, Canadians see themselves more as individuals within a group setting. Also the group has more permanence than it seems to have for Americans – Canadians see themselves as a less transient people, and more rooted to whatever community they adopt.

'Canadians are good at making and having fun too – perhaps because they have to. For instance, while Americans south of the border moan at the onslaught of the cold weather of winter, Canadians rejoice in it and have tamed it to their advantage. Cross-country skiing, skating, hockey or whatever activity, Canadians know how to adapt to their environment and vary their activities to suit the time of year and location accordingly – unrestricted by the more limited range of American pastimes. And they know how to throw a good party too! Canadians are convivial and know how to make outsiders feel welcome for themselves and not for what they represent.

'To be an American in Canada means fitting in with a similar, but subtly different, lifestyle and leaving behind some of the stronger identifications that Canadians find difficult to hold with the same intensity as Americans do – the sense of patriotism and the idea of universal conformity to a social idea, for instance. But these are not radical differences and these changes can often lead to rejoicing in a rewarding and refreshing change of pace and the slightly different outlook on life which sets Canadians apart from their American neighbours to the south.'

A Canadian in America

Mark is a computer software engineer from British Columbia who lives in a middle-of-the-road suburban estate in Seattle, Washington. He has lived in the United States since 1982, first in California, then in Washington state. He is married to an American. They have a two-year-old son. His views on America and Americans:

'Americans are easy and comfortable to live with, but it is not that easy to get to know them well. They adopt a veneer of civility, an appearance of openness and informality, but they are actually reserved, polite with their opinions and refrain from the controversial. You don't get to know them too well unless you spend some time trying to understand what they are thinking.

'Sports are very important. Canadians like sports too, but there seems to be a lot more interest in them in America. It is more an aspect of the social fabric there. American football, baseball – these subjects always crop up in casual talk and are an important social icebreaker.

'There is a strain of anti-Americanism among Canadians which might seem petty. Americans are largely ignorant of this feeling. Their attitude is one of benign neglect about Canada. They don't think much about how there might be something substantially different up north. People who have lived in only one country think we are all basically the same and, unless you have lived in both countries, you don't really see these differences.

'Many differences between Americans and Canadians are the result of important historical roots that run deep. America was created out of revolution, civil war and lofty ideals. They underwent lots of important character-building tests that Canada never did. Canada as a nation had no real sense of purpose, except not to be like its neighbour. As a result, it is less mature and less confident as a nation. The difference in national purpose and consciousness has been accentuated lately. Canadians have been wracked by national doubt – Meech Lake, Quebec separatism, the native Indian problem.

'There are also differences in government. There seems to be always some election going on in America. People vote for all kinds of positions – judges, sheriffs, sometimes even dog-catchers, are voted for. This seems to be a superficial difference at first but its importance grows with observation. Our systems of government differ, and this was something I came to fully understand only when I lived in America. In Canada, the party that is in power can push through any policy it wishes, such as the Goods and Services Tax which came into effect in January 1991 despite immense public opposition. In America, it is not 'winner takes all' in decision-making. Congress is not just a law-making, but a governing, body too. There may be a Republican president, but he has to deal with a Democrat-controlled Congress. Thus consensus is necessary. The government in power cannot really make any hard decisions without intensive scrutiny.

'I find Americans have a sceptical attitude towards government as a whole and a low degree of respect for government and government institutions. In Canada, government has a very prominent role in the development of the country and the Canadian business world is 'clubby', with established companies, influences and families. The climate for promoting business is much more centralised and institutionalised. Opportunities for a young graduate are not that great. Many jobs are in government or government-related institutions or companies that rely on government contracts. In the United States,

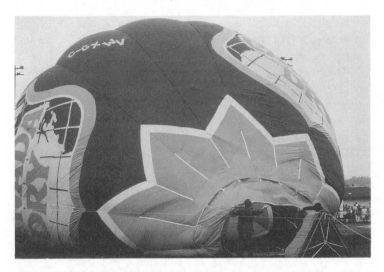

A hot air balloon advertises a brand of soft drinks which is obviously associated with Canada.

private industry has a bigger role to play in the social agenda. Because the country is more diverse, there are more localised spheres of influence and the local entrepreneur has greater opportunities. There is a greater diversity of opportunity in an economy that is so much larger, even though there is more competition too. For this reason, Canada has lost a lot of people it has educated. It has borne the educational cost while America is reaping the benefits.'

MADE IN CANADA

Think of America, and you think of Hollywood, apple pie, football. Think of Canada, and what comes to mind? Probably the maple leaf, ice hockey, sub-zero temperatures, the Mounties.

Canadians are generally annoyed when Americans take what were Canadian ideas and inventions and don't give due credit, when Americans think that many great ideas that originated from Canada were American originals. It is American ignorance of Canadian greatness that prickles the skin. To quote the editor of a Canadian magazine, *Châtelaine*:

'One of life's petty annoyances is how Americans co-opt but don't duly credit. In … an article [in an American magazine] purporting to track the genealogy of American humour, John Candy, David Steinberg, Rich Little, Mort Sahl, *Saturday Night Live* and SCTV figure prominently. Homegrown all right … in Canada. Elsewhere, an American writer claims Glenn Gould's daring and originality as "quintessentially in the American grain". *Harrumph.* And even Trivial Pursuit, which everybody knows is a made-in-Canada board game, was marketed in the States as an inalienable right: "Every American is entitled to Life, Liberty and the Pursuit of Trivia." *Double harrumph.*' (**Trivial Pursuit** was a game invented by Chris Haney, photo editor of the *Montreal Gazette*, and Scott Abbott, sportswriter for *Canadian Press*, in just 45 profitable minutes.)

For those of us who seem just as ignorant of Canadian examples of ingenuity, here are some made-in-Canada products:

- The **electron microscope** was developed by members of the Physics Department of the University of Toronto. The team was headed by Prof. E.F. Burton and included C.E. Howe, Ely Berton and James Hillier. Although the basic concept of the microscope came from Germany, it was Burton's team that eventually made it into a practical, commercial device.

- **Instant mashed potatoes**: Dr W.H. Cook, director of the division of bio-sciences at the National Research Council, was responsible for developing a new way of making frozen dried food. This turns potatoes, fish or meat into a powder which can be reconstituted with water to make croquettes.

- The first pre-cooked, vitamin enriched **baby cereal** was developed by doctors Frederick Tisdall, Theodore Drake and Alan Brown at the Hospital for Sick Children, Toronto, in the 1930s. It was first marketed internationally by Mead Johnson in 1930 as Pablum.

- The **gas mask** which saved the lives of so many Allied soldiers during World War I is an example of necessity being the mother of invention. It was developed by a Canadian doctor, Dr Cluny McPherson, when the German army released poison gas at Ypres in France in 1915. This first gas mask was one improvised with metal and cloth. It was gradually improved to become the standard mask for Allied soldiers.

- It is to Dr Gideon Sundbeck, chief engineer of the Lightning Fastener Company at St Catherine's, Ontario, that we owe thanks for keeping much of our clothing together. In the 1940s, Dr Sundbeck redesigned the old slide fastener to make the modern **zipper**. He also invented a series of machines for zipper manufacture. However, Dr Sundbeck was not the first man to think of the idea. This honour goes to an American, W.L. Judson, but he never succeeded in selling the idea.

- The **paint roller** is a simple invention, but it revolutionised the painting and decorating industry and did much to usher in the do-it-yourself era in home decorating. It was invented by Norman Breakey of Toronto in 1940.
- The **snowmobile**, or 'skidoo' as it is called, was invented by Quebec manufacturer Joseph-Armand Bombardier in 1922. The motorcycle-like machine has tracks like a tank that enable it to run on snow and ice, and is used for both recreation and work.
- The discovery of **insulin** for the treatment of diabetes was the work of four medical researchers at the University of Toronto – Frederick G. Banting, Charles H. Best, J.B. Collip and J.J.R. Macleod. Banting and Macleod were awarded the 1923 Nobel Prize for Chemistry, which they shared with their two colleagues.
- *Ghostbusters*, that box office comedy hit, was a product of Canadian filmmaker Ivan Reitman. Other Canadian films are *The Quest for Fire* and *Fiddler on the Roof* (directed by Canadian Norman Jewison).
- **Ice hockey** was invented by a group of soldiers in Kingston, Ontario, who tied blades to their boots and used field hockey sticks and an old lacrosse ball to keep boredom away one Christmas Day in 1855.
- **Basketball** was the invention of a Canadian, Dr James Naismith, who was an instructor at Massachusetts School. The need for a competitive indoor team sport led him to devise this game played under 13 basic rules with a ball and round hoops.

FAMOUS CANADIANS

Ask a non-Canadian to think of some famous Canadians and don't be surprised if he cannot recall the name of even one well-known son or daughter of this country. But in truth, there are many well-known Canadians although it is doubtful if many people realise the true nationalities of these people. One reason for this is that many Canadians have had to go south of the border where the opportunities to seek fame and fortune are greater by far. Consider, therefore, this list of famous Canadians whom most people think are Americans: former presidential adviser John Kenneth Galbraith; novelists Saul Bellow, Arthur Hailey, Jack Kerouac, Margaret Atwood, Stephen Leacock; Abe Rosenthal, executive editor of *The New York Times*; Mary Pickford, 'America's sweetheart'; actors Raymond Burr, Genevieve Bujold, Raymond Massey, Lorne Greene, Christopher Plummer, Donald Sutherland, William Shatner, Margot Kidder, Michael J. Fox (the all-American boy of the television series *Family Ties*); singer Paul Anka; and cosmetics queen Elizabeth Arden.

Of course, Canada has its heroes and heroines too and others who have left their mark on their various fields. References to many of them and thumbnail sketches are sprinkled throughout this book. In addition, here is a purely arbitrary list of more famous Canadians:

- Among the early Canadian books that give one a glimpse of the pioneer life are those written by two immigrant English women, **Susanna Moodie** and **Catherine Parr Traill.**

  Susanna was already a published author when she and her husband left England in 1832 to settle in the backwoods of Upper Canada. She describes the difficulties of pioneer existence, as experienced by an English lady used to the comforts of life, in her two most well-known books, *Roughing it in the Bush* and *Life in the Clearings*.

  While the pioneer life did not agree with Susanna, who returned with relief to a more civilised life after a few years in the bush, her sister Catherine had a more positive outlook. She undertook to give those who would follow her a 'survival manual' entitled *The Canadian Settler's Guide*, in which she describes how to grow corn, make your own soap and gather wild rice, among other things.

- A controversial figure, once considered a traitor to his country but now acknowledged as hero and martyr, is **Louis Riel**, a Métis born in 1844 in Manitoba. He was a deeply religious man, educated in

Montreal, who felt he was chosen to save his people and protect their rights. He led them in the Red River Rebellion and set up a provisional government but was forced to flee into exile in the United States when his revolution failed. He returned home when summoned to help lead his people in another revolt, the Northwest Rebellion, which also failed. Riel surrendered, was tried for treason and hanged in 1885.

- One of Canada's great landscape artists, **Emily Carr** was born in 1871 in Victoria, British Columbia. She studied art in San Francisco but had to turn her home into a boarding house and find other ways of making a living. She held her first major exhibition of paintings when she was 56 years old, when she was 'discovered' by the director of the National Gallery in Ottawa. Her paintings of the Coast Indians of British Columbia won her much recognition.

- Canada has a Chinese connection in **Norman Bethune**, a medical doctor from Ontario. He practised medicine in Montreal and served in the Spanish Civil War, where he organised the world's first mobile blood-transfusion service. Early in 1938, he joined the Eighth Route Army of the Chinese Communists in the hills of Yenan, where he formed the world's first mobile medical unit. He died in 1939 of an infection. Chairman Mao Tse-tung wrote an essay in which he extolled Bethune's 'boundless sense of responsibility', and the Chinese government donated a statue of Bethune which stands in downtown Montreal.

- The Bata shoe company, which is the world's largest manufacturer of footwear, was established by **Thomas J. Bata**, a Canadian. The company was actually founded by his shoemaker father in Czechoslovakia. Bata, an 11th-generation cobbler, moved it to Canada when he emigrated in 1939. Bata company now produces about 300 million pairs of shoes a year in 61 countries, supplies shoes in 115 countries and has 6000 retail outlets, many of them in the East. Bata directs these world operations from his headquarters in Batawa, Ontario.

- A recent Canadian hero is handicapped athlete **Terry Fox**. Fox was a 21-year-old track star who was stricken with cancer at the height of his career. In his courageous fight against the disease, he set out to run from one coast of Canada to the other in order to raise money for cancer research. It turned out to be his last event and he collapsed outside of Thunder Bay, Ontario, on September 1, 1983, and died nine months later. Every year since then, on the anniversary of his death, Canadians from coast to coast take part in Terry Fox runs to raise money for cancer research.

- Through radio and television, scientist **David Suzuki** has brought, and continues to bring, science into the homes of Canadians in a way that can be easily understood. He is especially noted for his TV series, *The Nature of Things*. He gained an international reputation when, as a professor of zoology at the University of British Columbia, he embarked upon a research programme on the common fruit fly and bred a strain that died in hot weather. His work caused him to be concerned about the effect that scientists have on the world. Science, he felt, was too important to be left to experts, so he set out to explain it to the public.

– Chapter Five –

THE TRUE NORTH

'With glowing hearts we see thee rise
The True North strong and free'

– from O Canada, the national anthem

According to Statistics Canada, the majority of Canadians live in cities. Over 75% of the population live in an urban rather than a rural setting.

This is a relatively recent phenomenon as Canada has strong rural roots. City dwellers, in fact, seem to belong to one of three groups: those whose ancestors moved to the developing cities as a lifestyle choice; those whose careers or occupations force them to live in urban areas; and newcomers to the country, used to cities in their native lands, who choose to band together with their ethnic counterparts in specific sections of Canada's largest metropolitan areas.

This has led to the population of Canadian cities becoming very cosmopolitan, and the diversity of food stores, restaurants and entertainment available in the three largest cities of Montreal, Toronto and Vancouver as well as some of the smaller ones – for instance, Winnipeg, Edmonton and Halifax – bears witness to this social mix.

CITY LIVING

Physically, Canada's cities resemble cities in many countries of the world. Relatively small central core areas, often dominated by high-rise office towers and expensive hotels, are surrounded by successive layers of residential communities, each with its own infrastructure and character, often extending several kilometres from the city centre but all linked by an intricate and efficient public transport system.

For those who live in these suburban areas, there is often less sense of identity with the city as a whole than with their specific part of it. This gives rise to a sort of geographic identity but in a way quite different from the social identity experienced in the close society of a small town or a rural community.

The city dweller is freed from one of the obligations that Canada's vast size imposes on those who live in the country – that of owning a car. Those who live in the cities have access to efficient urban transport – an extensive bus network that is often supplemented by a mass rapid transit system, such as the Montreal Metro, Vancouver Skytrain and Toronto TTC. In fact, many city dwellers choose not to own a car at all but to rent one on the relatively rare occasions when visits to friends, relatives or other family commitments take them out of the city.

Similarly, home ownership – often the ultimate dream for many Canadians – is not as common in a city where many live in rented

As most Canadian cities are modern and upbeat, the sight of two work horses passing by the Parliament buildings in Ottawa inevitably attracts much attention.

apartments in high-rise blocks, deterred from owning their own home by the high cost of real estate, taxes and maintenance.

Interaction with one's neighbours varies. Those in high-rise apartments tend to know little about and have little to do with their neighbours, except for those right next to them. In suburban housing estates, it is possible to have a nodding acquaintance with families who live on the same street.

Culture and the arts, often sadly lacking in the countryside and small towns, are a positive feature of the bigger cities. Symphony orchestras, theatrical experiences, dance and art provide city dwellers with an abundance of cultural opportunities. This is often cited as one main reason for choosing to live in a city.

All of Canada's major cities have professional sports teams too – there is usually ice hockey and Canadian football to watch in the winter months and baseball in the summer – and the frequency of their games makes avid fans out of many of the city's residents.

Other pastimes include shopping – for many Canadians more part of the culture than a simple necessity – visits to museums and art galleries and regular special events. All these are not available to the country or small-town dweller unless he is willing to make the long pilgrimage into the city and back for a specific event.

The development of a Canadian city lifestyle, relatively free of social obligations and with plenty of diversions, and tremendous employment opportunities have resulted in the shift to Canada's cities over the last 20 or 30 years.

But there are drawbacks to living in a city – rural and small-town values combined with a less hurried and relatively relaxed lifestyle and a strong sense of community are not easy to maintain in a city where the pace of life is faster and the community's sense of being responsible for the welfare of all its members is not as strong.

For those lucky enough to have a choice, living in the city has the appeal of convenience – but it means adapting to a lifestyle quite different from that of the smaller communities.

Toronto (Ontario)

Toronto, Canada's largest city, used to be nicknamed 'Toronto the Good' because it was a rather staid and uninteresting – if comfortable – place to live in. But few cities in North America have changed as much as Toronto in the last few decades!

The growth of the population over the last 50 years, with many people coming from different cultures and countries, has changed the city completely from the rather Anglo-Saxon oriented, complacent and dull place it was at the end of the last world war into a dynamic, multi-cultural metropolis of more than 3.5 million people.

Remarkably, however, this rapid change has not brought along many of the social ills which bedevil other major cities. Toronto remains one of the world's safest cities. Its transport system is efficient and fast, and its police force highly visible. Both these factors act as a strong deterrent to the various forms of personal attack becoming commonplace in other cities. The transport authority has even recently put in place a special programme in which suburban bus drivers have been authorised to let single women passengers alight directly outside their place of residence at night instead of having to walk there from the nearest bus stop.

The centre of Toronto is Bay Street, the financial heart of the country and the location of the country's largest stock exchange, the seventh largest in the world. Dominating the skyscrapers of Bay Street is the CN Tower, the world's tallest free-standing building, at the top of which a public viewing platform allows visitors to get a panoramic view of the city.

Other attractions include the historic Fort York and Casa Loma, and The Art Gallery of Ontario; its ethnic shopping and dining areas such as Chinatown and Kensington Market; its wide variety of permanent entertainment facilities, ranging from symphony concerts at Roy Thompson Hall to rock concerts at Ontario Place. Theatres, cinemas and sports events abound – the SkyDome is home to the city's popular baseball team, the Blue Jays – and there is plenty of green space within and close to the city for those who enjoy outdoor pastimes in winter and summer.

Toronto is a Huron Indian word meaning 'place of meeting' and, through all that it has to offer, Toronto certainly lives up to its name!

Montreal (Quebec)

Montreal is an intriguing combination of modern North American dynamism and old-world European elegance. Home to more than 3 million people, just slightly smaller than its Ontario rival, Montreal shares with Toronto its reputation for efficiency and safety, but adds a cultural ambience which is all its own.

In fact, Montreal's reputation internationally is as a very cosmopolitan city and it is its atmosphere which attracts visitors as much as its facilities. This is because it is very much a bilingual city and the home of a self-sufficient and thriving French culture. The way in which French and English cultures blend here is unique, and the recent addition of other ethnic influences from all around the world has made a visit to Montreal a truly special experience. In addition, Montreal has always had a reputation for good living, and the abundance of fine restaurants and cafés in its special 'quarters' help to keep this reputation alive.

Like Toronto, Montreal also has its share of historic places, museums, fine shopping areas, cultural activities and green spaces. Old Montreal, the Basilica of Notre Dame and McGill University are all worth a visit, as are the Montreal Museum of Fine Arts, the Place Ville Marie, the city's vast underground shopping centre, and Mont Royal Park in the centre of the city itself. The latter offers a fine panoramic view of Montreal and the St Lawrence River.

Despite having lost the title of Canada's largest city to Toronto, Montreal remains a major commercial and cultural centre, and the opportunity to experience its vitality and elegance is one no visitor to Canada should miss.

A close-up view of the Lions usually seen from the Lions Gate Bridge in Vancouver.

Vancouver (British Columbia)

Vancouver is the third largest city in Canada. In the beginning it was mainly populated by people of British ancestry, but with immigration over the years, Vancouverites are now of almost every race and colour. There is a huge Asian community, made up mostly of Chinese and including an increasingly visible number of Koreans and Vietnamese. Vancouver's Chinatown is the second largest in North America, next in size only to San Francisco's, and its restaurants serve a cuisine that, some would say, rivals even that of Hong Kong. There are also many Indians, mainly Sikhs, who have established a Little India along a section of Main Street where Indian groceries, spices, saris and restaurants can be found. For many new Asian immigrants, being able to buy their 'local foodstuff' is a great comfort in strange surroundings.

Originally a small sawmill town, Vancouver grew in importance and size when it became the westernmost terminus of the Canadian Pacific Railway, outstripping both the 'royal city' of New Westminster and the present provincial capital of Victoria.

The city spreads over the rich delta lands of the Fraser River, with a seascape and mountain backdrop that has given it a spectacular setting. Many parks and gardens abound in this beautiful city so that much of nature's beauty, peace and quiet is within easy reach of its residents. Perhaps the most spectacular of these green oases is Stanley Park, a heavily wooded area of more than 400 hectares (more than 1000 acres) right in the heart of the city. In summer, Vancouver's beaches are covered with sun lovers, although braver souls test their mettle by jumping into English Bay during the Polar Bear Swim, on cold January 1 every year.

The original nucleus of the city is Gastown, now a renovated tourist-oriented area of shops, restaurants and nightclubs, complete with charming cobblestone streets and old gas lamps. The heart of the city and its financial and business district is now further south, centred around Robson Square. Stately homes in Edwardian suburbs like Kerrisdale, Shaughnessy and Mount Pleasant contrast with high-income, high-rise apartment living in the West End.

There is an international airport, two universities – the University of British Columbia and Simon Fraser University – and a prestigious art school – the Emily Carr College of Art and Design. The city is home to the Vancouver Symphony Orchestra and its sporting heroes are the Vancouver Canucks (ice hockey) and BC Lions (Canadian football).

Vancouver is linked to the interior of British Columbia by the Trans-Canada Highway. Within the city, the excellent grid-like road network is supplemented by a public bus system and the mass rapid transit Skytrain.

Surrounding the core of the city are the municipalities that make up the metropolitan area known as the Lower Mainland. These are strung out along the delta of the Fraser River. North of the river, the mountains gradually close in and, as you travel east, the population centres of Pitt Meadows, Maple Ridge and Mission become less dense. The more open area to the south is made up of farms, interspersed with small communities such as those in the municipalities of Surrey, Langley, Abbotsford and Chilliwack.

SMALL-TOWN SNAPSHOTS

Despite the fact that 75% of Canadians are city dwellers, much of Canada is still country and small town in nature.

Many small towns are built around a single industry, such as fishing, logging or mining. Others might owe their existence to their strategic siting at the crossroads of rail or road communication. They are often separated from the next town by miles of open country, farm or ranch land.

The Canadian small town is easily recognisable. As you approach by road, you will often see a 'Welcome to Townsville, population 4000' sign. Often, there is an accompanying signboard listing the churches that are active in town – Anglican, Roman Catholic, Baptist, Full Gospel, Evangelical and so on. A third sign might display the badges of service clubs – Lions, Rotary, Kiwanis. Sometimes, a board will say 'This is a Block Parent community', meaning 'we look after our children here' (see *Canada's Young and Young at Heart*). All this gives the visitor the feeling that the small-town community is a close-knit and caring one.

On the outskirts of town, near the main highway, there is usually a cluster of service stations that serve passing motorists, while the road into town is lined with motels and hotels for the overnight traveller.

The centre of town often consists of one main street that might be no more than two blocks in length. Here you will find the general store, hardware store, drugstore, a couple of banks and perhaps some café-restaurants that often offer Chinese and Canadian 'smorgasbord' meals. The shopping mall is not quite as ubiquitous as you might expect but can usually be found in the larger towns. (One might even use it as a measure of whether a town has 'made it' in terms of size.)

The Charm of Being Small

The resident of a small town is often friendly and open, even to strangers. Unlike in the city, where the rush is always evident and people seldom pass the time of day with a stranger, there is time to stand and stare and comment upon the weather.

One of the pleasing features about living in a small community is the ease with which you get to know your neighbours – the cashier in the supermarket, the bank teller, post office clerk, sales attendant become more than familiar faces. You discover that the mother you

Small-town Canada with a relic of an earlier time.

THE TRUE NORTH

meet at a school function attends the same church as you. You see her again when your children join the gymnastics club. When shopping one day, she turns out to be the cashier at the supermarket check-out counter. Thus a web of relationships builds between you that forms the basis for a friendship. Walk around town, and chances are you will meet someone you know well enough to exchange a few civilities with.

The atmosphere in the town is usually casual, especially in summer, when the hot weather encourages the shedding of the many layers of clothing that were worn during winter. I once saw some guests at a wedding reception arrive in their bermudas.

Few people are in a hurry. There are no traffic snarls to fray the nerves, no horns being honked by impatient drivers. Pedestrians have right of way, and not only do they take it, they are also given it! You can stand at the street corner, waiting to cross, and a driver will stop and ask you to go. A car can pause in the middle of the road to let a passenger off, or two cars may halt the traffic while their drivers say hello. And those behind (granted, there is seldom more than one) will usually wait patiently until they are ready to move on again.

For the many people who choose to live here rather than in the city, these are the charms that more than make up for the lack of hustle and bustle, excitement and entertainment of city life.

Nevertheless, even a small-town resident sometimes looks for entertainment, so where does he find it?

Where the Action Is

Television is the standard recourse for most people when they need entertainment. In Canada, TV is not a toy for the indecisive for, with so many channels, the choice can be bewildering. Many households have at least two television sets and subscribe to cable television, enabling them to receive 25 channels or more. If that is not enough, you could instal a satellite dish in your back yard, and that would give you more than 100 channels to choose from.

84

Shopping is more of a necessity than a source of entertainment. There might be a shopping mall of sorts to spend the time in but, as has been mentioned earlier, it is not always a feature of a small town. Rather, this is a luxury to be indulged in when trips often taking an hour or more by road are made to bigger towns or cities nearby.

The local cinema offers second-run (and often second-rate) movies, and is often just a step from closure brought about by competition from more versatile video shops. Even in a small town, there is usually more than one video shop, offering cheap entertainment to residents. It has to be a good movie to entice one to pay something like C$7 at the cinema, when a video can be rented for just C$2 or C$3 a day.

As for culture and the arts, the town usually has a local choir, arts and theatrical group and a small gallery or two. The civic centre might occasionally host a performance by a visiting cultural group or symphony orchestra.

If you choose to do so, you can make your own entertainment by joining many organisations and activities. A look at the events page of the local newspaper will reveal a choice of something like this: Toastmasters Club, Overeaters Anonymous, Old Time Fiddlers, pottery classes, Weavers and Spinners Club, the community choir, outdoor association, Scottish Country Dance Club, Tai Chi Club, watercolour painting classes, Quilters Guild, Badminton Club, Rod and Gun Club, Karate Club, singles society, Calorie Counters, Bridge Club, scouts, guides and many others.

When the weather is fine, which is every season except winter, weekends see a proliferation of garage sales advertised in the classifieds section of the newspaper and on telephone poles all over town. Some people derive great enjoyment going from one garage sale to another looking for bargains.

Bingo games are another popular pastime. Hardly an evening goes by without a bingo game being conducted in some part of town. (More on garage sales and bingo games in *The Canadian Mosaic*.)

Many people who live in small towns are the kind who enjoy the country and the serenity of nature. Often, the great outdoors is right next to your home, or just a few minutes' drive away. It can be a local forest conservation area, where a few picnic tables and an outhouse are the only concessions to campers and picnickers, or it can be a national or provincial park complete with hot and cold shower facilities. The easy availability of outdoor activity often more than makes up for the lack of cultural activities or an exciting city life. You will find that practically every other house in town has an RV or recreational vehicle parked in the garage. This could be a camper, trailer or even a mobile home, or a boat and a 4x4 (four-wheel drive vehicle). The weekends are filled with such activities as fishing, camping, hiking and skiing.

Small Towns, East and West
Merritt

'Welcome to Merritt, a lake a day as long as you stay' – that's what the signboard tells visitors to this little British Columbia town of just about 6000 people.

Merritt is situated in the Nicola Valley, a high glacial valley about 600 metres above sea level. It is a two-and-a-half hour drive from Vancouver, at an important junction in the Coquihalla Highway which connects the west coast to the interior of the province. As you enter the town, lumber yards feature prominently and they fill the air with the fragrant scent of pine, fir and spruce.

The town grew as a result of coal and copper mining, but the forest industry is the big employer now – there are three sawmills in town. The valley itself is rich cattle country and many ranches surround the town. In fact, the first settlers were cattle ranchers, attracted by the vast grasslands of the valley. Many of Merritt's streets bear the names of the early pioneers, whose descendants continue to live in town.

But before the settlers came, the valley was home to many native Indian tribes. The valley was called after Chief N'Kwala, whose name was anglicised to Nicola. Today, there are five native Indian reserves

Remembrance Day parade in front of the Court House in Merritt.

in the area. In 1983, the natives formed the Nicola Valley Institute of Technology, based in Merritt. It is an independent institution for natives and non-natives and provides degree-level courses in agreement with other universities.

Tourism is carefully cultivated. Merritt's boast of 'a lake a day as long as you stay' is not an idle one as there are about 150 lakes and streams within the area, kept well stocked with salmon, trout and other fish. There are numerous trails along which to go hiking, horse riding, skiing and snowmobiling. The tourist information centre is staffed entirely by senior citizens who volunteer their time. Each Labour Day weekend in September, the Merritt Rodeo and Fall Fair provides local residents and tourists with the excitement of a rodeo, old time fiddling contests, pancake breakfasts and a community dance.

Campbellford
Set on the picturesque Trent Canal, Campbellford in Ontario has

A typical fall scene in small town Campbellford, Ontario.

about 5000 inhabitants, many of whose families have lived in the town for several generations.

The one main street, naturally called Front Street because it parallels the water, is intersected by the only other street of any significance, called also for obvious reasons Bridge Street. Together, these two form the downtown area: a collection of small locally-run shops with the post office, three banks and a liquor store thrown in for good measure.

Surrounding the downtown area, the majority of Campbellford's residents live in detached houses on other smaller streets, which also contain the town's facilities. For instance, Campbellford's ice hockey arena is tucked away at the back of the town behind the high school, on whose fields the other town teams practise whatever sport is currently in season. Adjacent to the arena and high school, the community hospital doesn't have a full-time doctor, but local physicians see their patients there and take turns to be on call for the relatively few emergencies which crop up. The town's many service clubs meet on different days – Rotary on Mondays, Kinsmen on Tuesdays and so on – and many of the town's prominent citizens and business people belong to several of them.

There are two small factories in Campbellford, both branches of American companies, but in the main, the economy of the town and its survival depend on the healthiness of the local area's small business and service ventures.

Most of the people here know each other – some of the town's doctors have brought several generations of the same family into the world and some of the teachers have taught them all too! So there aren't many secrets – indiscretions have an embarrassing way of surfacing no matter how hard one has tried to disguise them. But similarly, if there is someone in trouble, the community will always rally round to offer what support it can, be it financial, moral or social.

Campbellford has its local heroes – the scout leaders, the little league coaches, the leaders of the business community – and there is a strong community spirit in the town as a whole which epitomises small towns everywhere – a sense of local identity, lacking in the biggest cities of the country, and which keeps people in Campbellford and in towns like it all over the country. It is this sense of local community and spirit which is still to many the essence of Canada's strength and of its most important values – tolerance, understanding and moral uprightness.

COPING WITH THE SEASONS
Winter's Chill

Humorist Stephen Leacock once said that life in Canada consists of preparing for winter, enduring winter and recovering from winter. And, being Canadian, he ought to know.

Indeed, the seasons play an important part in the life of the people. As winter approaches, the householder must look critically at his home to winterise it. Storm windows and doors are checked, the central heating is turned on. Cars too must be winterised. Summer tyres are taken off and snow or all-weather tyres put on. The engine oil is changed to one of thinner viscosity.

Ranchers bring their cattle down from the hills. The Canada geese fly south and so do the 'snowbirds'. The 'snowbirds' (see *Canadianisms* in *Canadian Language*) are Canadians who fly south every year to Florida, Hawaii, Mexico and other sun-bathed lands to escape the grip of winter.

But winter does not mean the shutting down of everything, or the suffering of 'cabin fever' when one is kept indoors by the inclement weather for weeks at a time. Life still goes on and some things come alive only during this time of the year. A really beautiful winter's day, when the air is crisp and clear, the sky a cloudless blue and the snow sparkling in the sunshine, has to be experienced to be believed. One good way to deal with the winter's cold is to get outside and be active. Some Canadians love to spend time and money at ski resorts, while others will just take their winter entertainment wherever they can find it, cross-country skiing, sledding, skidooing, ice skating and ice fishing anywhere there is snow and ice. Frozen lakes are converted into ice-rinks by ice-skaters and are pockmarked with the little holes that have been drilled by the ice-fishermen.

In Canada, snow is everywhere during winter. The softly falling snow is a beautiful sight and can even be mesmerising. A snow-covered lawn is often an invitation to children and the young at heart to play, making snowmen and throwing snowballs at each other. Shovelling the driveway can be an enjoyable task (though some might not agree) and making a snowman requires more skill and experience than you might think. (Snow conditions have to be just right before a snowman can be built – the light powdery stuff may be what skiers look for, but a snowman needs snow that will stick together.)

Driving is particularly hazardous at this time of the year. When there is blowing snow, visibility on the highway can be cut down to a kilometre or less, ultimately producing a condition known as

Snow lends an air of serenity to this small village in Quebec.

'whiteout'. In such conditions, highway travel is extremely dangerous and roads may have to be closed. With snow and ice everywhere,
roads must be sanded to provide more traction for the tyres. The driver
must learn different skills, how to handle a slipping and sliding car
especially when the snow has been packed down into a layer of ice.
In fact, a driver new to such conditions might be wise to find some
open area like an empty car park to practise throwing his car into a
slide and regaining control of it so that he can drive more confidently.

'Black ice' is a particularly dangerous phenomenon on the highways. It occurs when there has been a sudden thawing or rain followed
by freezing temperatures. The water on the road freezes into a thin
layer of ice that cannot be seen, and a fast moving car loses all grip on
the road. There is little control so that the vehicle spins out of control
and may slide off the road into a ditch or onto the opposite side of the
road into the path of oncoming traffic.

Cracked or shattered windshields and headlamps are common when the sand and gravel that have been spread on the road to give your tyres traction become missiles to be flung at you by an overtaking car or truck.

Dressing in winter is an art that really can only be learnt when you are in the country. It is difficult to predict how cold a winter can be as this depends on which part of the country you are in. But it is safe to say that a visitor to Canada in winter must be prepared for temperatures below freezing.

Dressing in layers is often recommended, especially when you intend to exercise outdoors. You should wear top and bottom thermal underwear which is the first essential layer of clothing to put on. Its closeness to your skin helps you to keep warm. Unless you are going to the north, it need not be made of wool, which might be too warm and is often uncomfortably prickly to wear. Thermal clothing should be made of synthetic fabrics like polypropylene which will draw perspiration away from the body. (It may seem surprising, but it is possible to perspire profusely even though one is exercising in temperatures below freezing.) It is also essential to wear one or more knitted sweaters in wool or acrylic. Then top it off with a winter jacket, of which the warmest and lightest is made of down. It should be water- and wind-resistant. It is also important to keep your head covered with a hat or toque made of wool or synthetic fabric, as 60% of your body warmth is lost through the head. For the hands, gloves or mittens are important. Mittens are warmer as fingers are kept together and there is less surface exposed to the cold. Put your feet in wool or thermal socks and winter boots to keep them warm. A word about winter boots: it is better if they are slightly too large rather than too small, so an extra pair of socks can be slipped over for more warmth. Tight boots can restrict circulation and cause your feet to freeze. It is a bonus if the boots are also waterproof, as you will often be walking in snow or slush. Like winter tyres, the tread of your boots should provide good traction on icy pavements.

The air in winter is drier, and lips may crack and peel, skin become dry and flaky. Lip balms and moisturising creams for the skin are necessary. The hot, dry air that is circulated throughout the house with central heating compounds the problem. So too does the hot water that you use to wash your hands. But aside from the cold, dryness and wind, one culprit that is seldom recognised is the winter sun, whose ultraviolet rays can damage the skin. If you enjoy outdoor winter sports, you should use a sun block cream for protection.

But do not, however, get the impression that in Canada, one must always be heavily laden with clothes in winter. The above is only for times when you venture outdoors, and even then it depends on how cold it actually is. Indoors, you can wear as little as you wish, because of the 'miracle' of central heating.

Central heating makes even the harshest Canadian winter bearable. With it, you can stand at the window looking out on the knee-deep snow in your yard, yet be dressed in your summer shorts because the temperature in your house can be kept as high as you wish. (Of course, it would cause a heatwave in your heating bill.) Over the years, Canadians have experimented with various forms of heating their houses, from simple fireplaces in each room to the most ingenious methods of creating and spreading heat from one source through the house, without having to sit in front of the radiator, burning your front and freezing your back. By far the most common system nowadays involves a furnace, usually located in the basement of the house, connected by an extensive network of internal hot air ducts to all areas that need warmth in winter.

These furnaces are powered by various sources of energy. Some use electrical power (usually expensive), some oil (expensive too and sometimes subject to fluctuations in supply) and some natural gas (usually the cheapest, but not always available). Wood furnaces, sometimes in combination with one of the other sources, are also quite common, especially in the countryside, for obvious reasons of supply. Wood stoves, refined and developed from the primitive models used by Canadian pioneers, are also popular for providing supplementary heat to individual rooms in a house, as are localised electric forced air and baseboard heaters. A more recent source, which is gaining more popularity with Canadians, is the heat pump which draws heat directly from outside the house (interestingly enough even in winter, there is always some heat residual either in the air or in the ground) and re-circulates it through the internal ducts.

Whatever the source, however, central heating has become a must and it would be extremely rare to find a house or apartment in Canada that is not equipped to deal centrally with the cold blasts of winter.

Signs of Spring

When it's late January and early February, most people will have had their fill of winter and will be looking for signs of spring.

Spring is in the air – what does that mean? It could mean that when you are out walking, you suddenly notice that the bare branches are starting to bud again. Others look for birds, and the first sight of a robin in the yard is often occasion for joy. Ranchers can tell that the cold weather's done when their cows start calving.

And it is not just nature that tells you spring is just around the corner. Shop window displays also change with the seasons. Snow shovels give way to bicycles and racks of seed packets. Clothing stores put away their winter jackets and offer summer blouses and T-shirts. Every now and again, you see someone on a bicycle. Shorts and skirts are in vogue again. The first advertisement for a garage sale is also a definite sign that warmer times are here. The impatient gardener will take every opportunity of sunshine to clear the dead leaves and winter debris to ready his yard for the next season's plantings.

For a more authoritative opinion as to whether you've seen the last of the snow, wait for Groundhog Day on February 2. On that day, everybody watches with bated breath for a special little groundhog called Wiarton Willie, who lives in Wiarton, Ontario, to come out of his hole. The belief is that if it is a bright sunny day and Willie sees his shadow, he will jump back in again, and winter will remain for another six weeks. Willie's predictions, however, have to be taken with a pinch of salt, as his accuracy rate is rather low.

The change in the seasons is usually a time of rain and wind. March and April are cold, wet and windy months. Spring season is mud season. Thawing ice makes mud slides and very bumpy roads and pot holes. Drivers must be careful. Thaws can make many places very muddy and bog a car down in a back road.

Long, Hot Summer Days

It often comes as a surprise to learn that Canadian summers can be really hot. Somehow, one's picture of this northern country is that of constant cold and ice and snow. However, except for the North, other parts of Canada can experience fairly warm summers because of the intrusion of tropical air from the Gulf of Mexico and the hot deserts of the American southwest. Some days in the months of June, July and August can even be tropically hot and humid.

The days are long. The sun rises as early as 4 a.m. and does not set until after 10 p.m. Those who can, take advantage of these long warm, sunny days to be outdoors. Gardens blossom. There are activities like camping, hiking, fishing, baseball, tennis, golf ... the list goes on and on; so many reasons to hurry home from work every Friday, to take off for that cottage by the lake.

The smell of summer is the smell of steak grilling on a barbecue pan. Increased outdoor activity is echoed by the renewal of nature. Flies emerge as if from nowhere, and the swarms of mosquitoes and blackflies can make life a misery. There are literally clouds of these little insects, especially in wooded campsites, all through May and well into June.

Schools close from the end of June to the end of August, and this is the long summer break for most families who go on holiday at this time of the year. Community and all other organised group activities take a break too, because there is seldom anyone around to participate.

Fishing: a favourite pastime of Canadians.

For many Canadians, especially those who live in apartments, summer brings a longing for a way of life that cannot be found in the towns and cities and for which proximity to water is an absolute necessity. This explains the phenomenon of the 'summer cottage', a home away from home that is a prized possession of many families. Some cottages have been in the same family for several generations, and some change hands regularly, but they all share the same basic purpose: to allow their owners to get away from the hurried pace of their ordinary lives and spend time in water-based leisure pursuits – fishing, canoeing, water-skiing, sailing or simply sitting around enjoying the sun and watching the surrounding flora and fauna.

After Labour Day, the unofficial end of the summer season, most cottages are left unvisited, though the ritual of closing and securing them for the winter months is a long and elaborate one. However, there has been a trend in recent years to winterise some of the larger cottages, so as to be able to stay there all year round.

Autumn Colours

Summer's heat is tempered now, but the days are still sunny and warm, and the nights sharply cool. The trees take on the loveliest colours of flaming reds, deep browns and vivid gold. But the planting season is almost over, and it is time to clear the weeds and leaves.

Some people are depressed by the dying back of nature, and the shorter days. By late October and especially in November, the shorter days really begin to affect one's life. Children leave for school in the morning when it is still dark, and office workers come home after the sun has set. It can be rather depressing if you come from the tropics and are used to a fairly even distribution of 12 hours of light and 12 hours of darkness all year round. It gets dark very early in the afternoon, and when you come home from work it can be pitch black outside. Although it is only 5 p.m., your instinct tells you that it's already late, and you should have had your dinner and gone to bed.

LIVING IN THE NORTH

When Canadians speak of 'the North', they generally mean the Northwest Territories and the Yukon, areas north of the 60th Parallel. These two territories are not as economically developed or heavily populated as the provinces to the south, and living in the North has its own special requirements.

In the Northwest Territories, 22% of the population or about 14,000 people live in Yellowknife, the capital of the territory and the centre of government. It is on the extreme southern edge of the area. Transport in and around Yellowknife is good and prices are relatively low. Iqaluit (Frobisher Bay), Hay River, Inuvik and Fort Smith are towns with more than 2000 people.

In the Yukon, about three-quarters of the people live along the Alaska Highway. Whitehorse, the capital, has about 20,000 people, and Dawson City, the second largest town, has about 1600 residents.

The rest of the population live in villages and small settlements of a few hundred people, almost always very isolated. In the Yukon, there are also 'company towns' in which the population depends upon a mining company for jobs and municipal facilities.

Travel into these areas is by air, and often one has to catch as many as four or five planes (each time a smaller one) to get there. Commercial air carriers operate scheduled services to most communities and charter services everywhere else. Almost everything has to be air-freighted, a very costly method of transport, and food and other necessities are therefore outrageously expensive.

The average weekly cost of food for a family of four in Yellowknife, Northwest Territories, and Whitehorse, Yukon, is about C$160, compared with C$123 average weekly cost for the whole of Canada. A friend who lived in the North for six months said a litre of milk cost about C$4, a small loaf of bread C$6, and apples cost C$1 a piece. The local people consequently eat 'country food'. This means game like moose, beaver, rabbit, fish, caribou and bear and little else. The Inuit live almost exclusively on meat and fish and fowl. The Dene eat some vegetables and grain, but very little.

Most of these small settlements do not have the rudimentary services that Canadians in the south take for granted. There is seldom any hotel or motel, no café or restaurant. But there is usually a school and some sort of library, a mounted police detachment and several churches. Groceries, clothing and other supplies are often sold by Northern Stores, the successor to the Hudson's Bay Company. Health services are the responsibility of a nurse, supplemented by occasional visits from a doctor. A dentist and an optometrist may visit several times a year. A patient requiring major medical treatment must be flown out to Yellowknife, Inuvik or Edmonton.

Housing is standard, provided by the federal government under the Homeowner's Assistance Programme. Although almost every community has electricity, provided mainly by local diesel generating units and sometimes by hydroelectric power, only a few have running water. Water comes from wells or is trucked in. Sanitary facilities are inadequate and modern conveniences such as a flush toilet are scarce. Sewage disposal systems are rare because of the difficulty of keeping sewers from freezing. Houses either have a holding tank with a pump-out service, or more often, what is euphemistically termed 'honey buckets', in which sewage is collected in plastic bags which are then picked up and trucked to a dump.

Alcohol abuse is a problem in the North, especially with the native people, and much of the police work has to do with alcohol-related problems. Because of this, some communities prohibit the import of alcohol, and anyone wishing to buy liquor in such 'dry communities' must apply for a permit.

When driving north, the motorist must prepare himself for conditions that are quite unlike those in any other part of Canada. Northern roads are characterised by long distances and infrequent traffic. Most all-weather roads have gravel surfaces and parts of some major highways, like the Alaska Highway, Klondike Highway and Hay River Highway, are paved.

The main highway into the Yukon is the Alaska Highway, built during World War II. Other major roads in the Yukon are the Robert Campbell Highway, the Klondike Highway, the Dempster Highway which links the Yukon with the Northwest Territories, and the Top-of-the-World Highway running west into Alaska.

The principal highway of the Northwest Territories is Mackenzie Highway. It provides a link with Alberta in the south, while the Liard Highway is NWT's road link with British Columbia.

Because of the long distances one has to travel between communities, weather forecasts and information on road conditions are regularly given on the radio. Nevertheless, whether you are driving north in winter or summer, survival equipment is important. Your vehicle must be in good condition. You should carry a tow rope or chain, at least one spare tyre, an axe, a box of matches, tools, first aid kit, fan belts and fuses. Extra gas (as petrol is known in Canada and the United States) and oil are necessities as gas and service stations are few and far between. Bringing extra food like chocolate bars, canned food and fruit is also a good idea. If you are travelling in winter, add a snow shovel to your emergency equipment, a good winter coat, mitts, a sleeping bag and some blankets. In summer, you should have insect repellent and water.

How Cold Is the North?
Nowhere else in Canada does climate rule human activities as in the North. The type of housing, work patterns, leisure activities and transport are all largely determined by weather conditions.

Winters are cold and long, with temperatures in February averaging between -15°C and -30°C. Low temperatures (it is not uncommon for temperatures to fall below -40°C) and strong winds produce what the weather forecaster calls a 'wind-chill factor' that creates severe, sometimes dangerous, winter conditions for people.

Most outdoor activity and movement come to a halt when there is a blizzard – snow or blowing snow – and visibility is cut down to less than a kilometre. Fog is another problem, especially in summer in the Arctic islands, when the presence of open water creates high humidity. In winter, ice fog is a common occurrence because of the freezing of warm, moist air from buildings and vehicle exhaust fumes.

But in the summer months, it averages 12°C to 13°C south of the tree-line to 3°C to 8°C in the Arctic islands. Warm air currents from the Pacific Ocean can even make the mercury rise above 25°C in some parts of the Yukon and the Mackenzie Valley.

FROM LOG CABIN TO TRAILER HOME
The very earliest Canadian homes, if you discount the tents and tepees of the native peoples, were made from logs that the first settlers had hewn from the giant forests around them. Log buildings served as churches, mission posts, trading stores, family homes and shelters of every kind. Today, in spite of the many alternative materials that are

available to the builder, log houses are still prevalent on farms and ranches and as holiday retreats in the country because they are recognised as strong, durable and beautiful structures that are in harmony with their natural surroundings. Log house building, far from being a dying tradition, seems to be holding its own in a world where steel, plastic and glass are the universal building materials and wood, where it is found, has first to be chipped, stripped and otherwise treated before it is used. Canadian log homes have even found a niche in the export market. Several, often small, companies, have found it viable to first construct these homes log by log, then dismantle them for shipping and reassembling in Japan especially, where log homes are a popular trend.

Canadian suburban houses, however, are more standard looking, with the wooden frame house being more common than that of brick. Construction of the frame house usually begins with digging for a foundation of concrete to be poured. A skeletal framework made of wooden planks forming the walls of the house is then erected on the concrete base. The frame is covered with sheets of plywood on the outside and gypsum board on the inside to complete the walls. These walls sandwich a fibreglass material that serves as insulation against the cold. The external plywood wall is commonly covered with vinyl or wooden siding, and sometimes a brick veneer, purely for cosmetic purposes. Unlike a brick house, the wood frame house can be completed in as a short a time as three months.

Often a real estate developer will just clear the land and divide it into building lots. The buyer, after purchasing his empty land, has many options as to how he wishes to get his dream house built. He can employ a draughtsman or an architect to custom-design his house, or choose a ready-made building plan, available from magazines and books and building companies. If he is a true do-it-yourself handy-man, he can take on the job of building from start to finish himself, without help from a professional builder. Alternatively, he may hire a builder to take the house up to a specific stage, such as seeing that

Building a wood-frame house. It takes just a few minutes to nail a wall together and erect it.

the excavation, foundation and framing of the structure are done, after which he can take over and finish the job. He can also hire a builder to take the job from start to finish, but supervise the work himself. His most expensive option would be to hire an architect to take charge of the entire project, from the designing to completion of the house.

The house may have just a single level, or two or three levels, in which case the bottom-most storey is called the basement and can be below or at ground level. If the house stands by itself, it is a single detached house. Although it can vary from neighbourhood to neighbourhood, most suburban properties tend to blend into one another, that is, front lawns often merge and there are no fences or gates to separate one property lot from another. Where there are fences or hedges defining the property line, they tend to be low and decorative. Back fences are generally higher and more protective of privacy.

Houses that are attached to another are sometimes called 'townhouses' and may be further distinguished by other names – a duplex (two houses attached to each other on one side, or semi-detached houses), a four-plex (four houses attached together), or six-plex (six houses attached to each other) and so on. The term condominium housing or 'condos' refers to high-rise apartment buildings or rows of low-rise buildings.

In 1990, a US-based real estate company conducted a survey on the prices of similar type executive homes and apartments in 46 cities around the world. The accommodation was the type likely to be bought or rented by an executive with an annual income of C$170,000. The survey found that in Tokyo, a 150-square-metre three-bedroom executive home sold for about C$1.17 million; in London, an executive home cost an average of C$827,000; but in Toronto a 225-square-metre four-bedroom home cost an average C$526,000, while a similar home in Edmonton could be bought for an average of C$222,000.

Within Canada, figures of the 1986 Census showed that Ontario homes had the highest average estimated value of C$104,000, followed by second-highest values in British Columbia with C$98,850, and Alberta with C$84,900. Among the big cities, homes in Toronto had the highest average estimated value of C$142,000, followed by Vancouver with C$127,000, Ottawa-Hull with $116,800, and Victoria with $103,000. It is safe to assume that prices are much higher now.

In 1986, the householder spent an average of C$720 on the cost of shelter per month (for mortgage payments, essential utilities, heating costs and property taxes), while for a renter, the average monthly shelter cost was C$430.

Renting or Buying a House?

Federal housing policy in Canada is mainly the responsibility of the Canada Mortgage and Housing Corporation (CMHC), established in 1946 to administer the National Housing Act. The CMHC works with the provinces to ensure that all Canadians have access to adequate housing at an affordable cost. The assistance may take the form of loans made, often at reduced interest rates, for the construction of affordable rental accommodation for low- and middle-income families and the elderly.

There are also special loans to homeowners and landlords to help renovate and bring deteriorating housing up to minimum standards.

It is possible to discover which houses are for sale by just driving around housing estates. Those houses which are on the market often have 'For Sale' signs displayed on their lawns. Some of these signs may say the house is 'For Sale By Owner' or the signs may belong to one of many real estate companies operating in the area. Another good way of finding a house to buy or rent is to go to a real estate agent who will have a listing of most of the properties that are available in his district. Although there are many different real estate companies, they all have access to the same pool of available properties that are listed for sale or rent.

Some of the standard features that are included in houses for sale are cupboards, clothes closets, plumbing and electrical wiring. Sometimes, refrigerators and other appliances like kitchen stoves and dishwashers may be included. Electricity for lights, radio and television and other small household appliances is supplied at 110 volts.

Rents may include heating costs, hot and cold water supply, and sometimes electricity and gas, and household appliances like kitchen stove, refrigerator, washer and dryer.

In your search for a home, you might come across condominiums with a sign that says the housing is 'adult oriented' or one that might say 'seniors preferred'. These are apartments reserved only for older people, who prefer to keep a quiet pace of life and not have it disrupted by crying babies or children playing in the yard. Families with young children are not welcome to rent these apartments. Similarly, some apartment building owners do not allow pets.

Trailer homes are a form of low-cost housing. Having said this though, it must be noted that costs can vary considerably depending on the amenities that are included in the home. A trailer park is one where you can rent a trailer home (which looks like a large container) already on site. Some people have their own trailers and rent a pad in the park on which to put their 'house'. Many of the families who live in these trailer parks are in the lower-income bracket and tend to be transient in nature, moving to towns where they can find work. Retired elderly people who do not wish to be encumbered with a large house and garden at this time of their lives also form a large part of trailer park residents. They spend a fair amount of their time in an RV (recreational vehicle) travelling around the country or travelling south to escape the cold.

– Chapter Six –

CANADIAN LANGUAGE

Because of its unique heritage and composition, Canada is in reality a country of many different languages. Travel through the breadth of the country and you will hear a variety of native languages (Cree, Ojibwa, Iroquois etc.) as well as the widest possible range of languages imported into the country with early immigrants and still widely spoken in ethnic pockets through the country. German, Dutch, Spanish, Ukrainian, Polish, Tamil, Hindi and Chinese in all its dialects can still be heard somewhere in the country, and all contribute to the rich linguistic mix of Canada as a whole. Officially, however, Canada is a country of two languages, services in either of which are accessible to all its citizens no matter where they live. However, neither the French nor the English spoken in the country is exactly the same as the language spoken today in their countries of origin, as they have changed and evolved on their own. The two Canadian languages have acquired a distinct character over time, and to the practised ear, they identify the nationality of their speakers just as clearly as the maple leaf flag pins which Canadians abroad often wear in their lapels.

THE ENGLISH CANADIAN LANGUAGE

So how can you tell if the stranger you are talking to is a Canadian by his speech? Here are the secrets.

Most people will tell you that the most tell-tale giveaway in Canadian speech is the addition of 'eh' at the end of a remark, as in 'Is that right, eh?' or 'How y're doing, eh?' This is true for a lot of people, but if you think this method will enable you to instantly identify the speaker as a Canadian the first time he opens his mouth, you're in for a disappointment. Not all Canadians speak like that, and even those who do, don't do it all the time. So take this advice with a pinch of salt, eh?!

In fact many features of Canadian English can also be found in either British or American English, and it is probably this very combination of both which really distinguishes the English spoken in Canada. For example, a Canadian will use the American words 'fall, French fries or garbage can' rather than the British terms 'autumn, chips or dustbin'. But interestingly enough he will also often say 'tap' rather than 'faucet'. The spelling of Canadian English usually follows the British rather than the American model too, e.g. 'colour' not 'color', and 'centre' not 'center'.

But these are only generalisations and there are many other factors to take into account in analysing Canadian English, such as regional and ethnic differences. Newfoundlanders, for instance, speak English with an accent quite different from their Ontario counterparts, while a family with a strong European background may pronounce the same word differently from one with a Chinese background. There have been many learned attempts to define Canadian English and to attempt to standardise it, but as it is still constantly changing, its nature remains a subject for disagreement. There are, however, dictionaries which deal with Canadian English, such as *The Gage Canadian Dictionary* and *A Concise Dictionary of Canadianisms* which can be consulted if you are in doubt about the proper word to use.

Apart from the British and American influences, there are also some words and expressions which have arisen from circumstances peculiar to being in this country, and yet others which have been borrowed from people of native and other origin. In fact, the name Canada itself was probably derived from *kanata*, a Huron-Iroquois word for village or small community. It was first recorded by French explorer Jacques Cartier in his journal and referred to the St Lawrence area, but was later adopted as the official name for the new country.

English Canadianisms

There are some words which are not exclusively Canadian, either in origin or in usage, but which you'll certainly hear often enough in Canada:

- 'Huge', 'enormous' and 'gigantic' are all big words for a very big country. But none of them seems to be big enough for Canadian purposes, so try '**humongous**' – that appears to be a particularly Canadian way of describing the vastness of the country.
- At the other end of the scale, try using '**tad**' to describe something that's just a little bit of whatever, such as being 'a tad out of line'.
- If you go to the Canadian north, you'll certainly come across '**muskeg**', swampy or marshy land that goes on for miles and miles: an Algonkian Indian word which has been adopted into the English Canadian language.
- While up north you might find yourself eating '**pemmican**' or '**bannock**'; the first being dried meat, often rather tough and

stringy, and the second relating to the traditional flour and water pancakes guaranteed to keep hunger at bay anywhere you go.

- Coming further south, visit southern Alberta or British Columbia and experience the '**Chinook**', a dry warm wind that blows from the southwest. During winter, it often causes a sudden warming of temperatures that melts the snow into unwelcome slush.

- And speaking of wintertime activities, what about '**curling**'? Not something you do in bed with a good book, but a winter sport which enjoys tremendous popularity among Canadians. Played on ice, it is a little like lawn bowling, as two teams compete against each other to slide special smooth stones (called '**rocks**') down the ice, trying to get their rock closest to the tee in the centre of the target area.

- Another winter word is '**black ice**', which forms on the roads when rain or a slight thaw is followed by freezing temperatures, turning the water into a transparent sheet of ice which cannot be seen by drivers. Many a winter accident has been caused by black ice.

- Canadian winters also introduced the '**toque**', a knitted woollen cap, indispensable for keeping your head warm in the freezing temperatures of January and February.

- And finally Canadian winter creates the '**snowbirds**', not always of the feathered variety, but as a term often used to describe the human cousins of the snow geese who migrate in their recreational vehicles or on the planes of Air Canada to warmer temperatures in Florida or California during the winter months.

There are lots of other Canadianisms which you will hear in common usage, ranging from the word '**hydro**' used to describe both the electricity supply and the company which provides it; '**medicare**', the government health insurance plan; a '**chesterfield**' on which you sit (you might want to call it a sofa); and finally '**zip**' or '**zilch**', which means absolutely nothing at all!

LANGUAGE AND 'THE TWO SOLITUDES'

Depending on where you live in Canada, it is easy to forget that there is not one official language, but two. English is the most frequently used, but there are large sections of the country in which French is the mother tongue and English very much a second language. In 1945, one of Canada's most well respected authors, Hugh MacLennan, wrote a now famous novel about this aspect of the Canadian experience and its effect on the relationship between the two linguistic groups, calling it *The Two Solitudes*. MacLennan, at that time a professor of English Literature at McGill University in Montreal, attempted to analyse the nature of Canadian society and to reflect upon its divisions through a fictionalised account of the English/French tensions in Quebec at the time of World War I. *The Two Solitudes* caused much controversy at the time of its publication, and although events in Canada have changed many of the opinions in MacLennan's book, the issues of division between the French and English cultures are still debated in the Canada of today. In fact, MacLennan's phrase, 'two solitudes', is still used to describe the nature of the relationship between the French and the English, and MacLennan, who died in 1989, is still remembered as one of the first prominent Canadian literary figures to draw attention to the need for all Canadians to regard themselves as part of one complete entity rather than submerge themselves in regional differences.

FRENCH AND ENGLISH

According to the census of 1986, more than 6 million people, or 25% of the total population, use French as their native tongue (62% are native English speakers), with the main concentrations being in Quebec, New Brunswick and some parts of Nova Scotia, Newfoundland, Ontario and Manitoba.

The federal government, which has often been headed by a French Canadian prime minister, has been increasingly aware during this century of the divisions which can be caused by ignoring or mishan-

Signposts to everywhere at Signal Hill in St John's, Newfoundland. The names of the world's cities are in English and French, the two official languages of Canada.

dling the importance of the French language to its native speakers – particularly those in Quebec. As a result, after many decades of ill feeling over language issues, an Official Languages Act was passed in 1969, declaring that English and French had equal status in Canada, and that all services throughout the country were to be provided for all citizens in both of these languages.

Thus today, from the box of cereal on your breakfast table to any other product you buy in Canada, the information and advertising are in both official languages, no matter where in the country you buy it. All federal government forms have a French and an English side, and all federal offices are equipped to provide public services in either language.

However, you don't have to speak both languages yourself to get by in Canada. Currently only about 4 million of the 27 million Canadian population are bilingual – most of them in Quebec – although this number is increasing all the time, through various special language programmes. The most widespread of these is French immersion, a type of schooling in which students are taught all – or some – subjects entirely in the other language than that which they speak. Pioneered in 1965 in the English-speaking community of St Lambert, Quebec, among kindergarten students, the concept of French immersion has spread widely throughout the country and is now a common part of school systems in nearly all provinces. The idea of teaching a second language by total immersion in it when young has been internationally recognised as a successful concept, and graduates of French immersion courses have found that their language skills are much in demand in an increasingly bilingual Canada.

CANADIAN FRENCH
The French spoken in Canada – mostly in Quebec – is for the greater part very similar to the French spoken in France. It is not a dialect nor a patois, as it shares France's linguistic heritage and is an integral part of international French.

However, there are also differences between France's French and that of Quebec. Both the geographical situation and the historical and socio-cultural North American context have given birth to linguistic forms which are called 'quebecisms'. The term 'quebecism' refers to words that are peculiar to Quebec such as *motoneige, âge d'or, char, epluchette, dépanneur, souffleuse, tabagie* and *barbier*. In order to contribute to the collective growth of French language in Canada, and to facilitate communication between French-speaking peoples, the Office de la Langue Française du Quebec has the responsibility for officially accepting such 'quebecisms'.

French universities in Quebec do considerable research in linguistics and terminology. Jean Claude Corbeil, a linguist and terminologist at the University of Montreal, and Claude Poirier, linguist and lexicographer at Laval University, are well known for their contributions to the French language.

HERITAGE LANGUAGES

Slightly over 13% of the population speak neither English nor French as their native tongue. Two-thirds of these 3 million people speak a language of European origin, such as Dutch, German or Polish. However, since the 1960s the use of Asian and Middle Eastern languages, especially Chinese, Vietnamese, Punjabi, Hindi and Urdu, has grown considerably.

This fact too has been acknowledged by the government and the provincial education systems, many of which now have heritage language programmes in the schools to ensure that these native languages survive in a multi-cultural Canada and are not swamped by the all-pervasive use of English or French. Unlike the United States, Canada is actively trying to preserve its multi-lingual, multi-ethnic and multi-cultural society and, at the same time, mould the population into one people with a common outlook on their country and the world. It is a very difficult task, but preserving language is a very important component of its success.

BODY LANGUAGE

Non-verbal communication in Canada is not really different from that used in most other societies whose background is culturally English. Those who have some familiarity with both the polite – and not so polite – gestures made by both Englishmen and Americans will find most of them in use in Canada fairly commonly, and will have no trouble interpreting their meanings. For those not so familiar with western culture, it is probably best to beware of non-verbal gestures at first, as there are some significant differences between those used in non-western cultures and those in use in Canada, and an over eager use of a particular gesture (unless you are absolutely sure of its meaning) could lead to embarrassment. However, there are several excellent books available for those people who want to bone up on this area, and the best thing to do to thoroughly understand body language in Canada would be to read one of them. The very best of these is probably the one called simply *Gestures*, the result of a long and thorough study of the subject taken all over the world by renowned anthropologist Desmond Morris and his two co-authors, and published by Stein and Day publishers of New York in 1980.

LONG DISTANCE LANGUAGE

Canadians statistically use the telephone more than any other nation on earth and it would be a rare house which did not have a telephone in this day and age. After all, the inventor of the telephone was himself a Canadian, and his legacy certainly endures in his adopted country. Born in 1847, Alexander Graham Bell came to Canada from Scotland with his parents in 1870. Originally trained as a speech therapist like his father, Bell first settled in Brantford, Ontario, and spent much of his time working on a device that would help his speech-impaired clients communicate more clearly with one another. In 1876, during the course of one such experiment, Bell uttered the immortal words 'Come here Watson, I need you' into his end of the speech device and the telephone was born. Bell patented the Bell Telephone, revolution-

ising long distance communications and leading to the opening of the first commercial telephone exchange in 1878.

Telephone services today are provided through various public and private companies, the biggest of which is appropriately named Bell Canada. These various telephone companies own and maintain the telephone lines throughout the country and have different plans for their use, which they offer to their customers. The basic rule of thumb is that local calls – within a designated area – are free while those going further afield are charged according to distance. Most communities in North America are now accessible to one another through direct dialling and many countries of the world can also be reached via satellite by simply dialling the telephone number without any need to resort to an operator. Special services are also offered by the telephone companies, including service for the deaf and a variety of public information services. Fax machines have recently become very popular in Canada, and these too can be used on the regular telephone lines.

Getting a telephone installed is not a complicated process either. In most areas, phones will be installed within a day or two of being requested, and all lines are private in the major areas. In addition to renting their lines, the telephone companies also sell and service equipment, but they no longer have a monopoly on doing so. The telephone user now has a number of options as to what equipment can be bought and installed, and there are many retail outlets that sell a range of telephone instruments and other telephone related merchandise.

By contemporary standards telephone service in Canada is not expensive. Most families will have a basic telephone bill that runs to about C$20 to 25 per month for service and equipment with the long distance portion of the bill depending on the time, distance and duration of the calls made. Using the telephone is very much a part of the Canadian lifestyle – which may be one of the reasons why the Canadian postal service has fallen on hard times in recent years!

– Chapter Seven –

GETTING AROUND IN CANADA

Because of its vast size, moving from place to place in Canada has always been a major undertaking. As a result, ways of moving about inside the country have changed and evolved just as the country itself has done. The transition from canoes, sleds and pack animals to the sophisticated air, rail, road and sea services that now link Canada together has been a long and complicated one, and not without its problems. But modern Canada now boasts a transport and communications system which is another factor that cements the various regions into a unified whole.

THE HEYDAY OF CANADIAN RAILWAYS

Many historians have commented that Canada was built by the railway. Canada as a country was itself created by the joining of the older, well-established provinces in the east with the former colony of British Columbia in the west through the building of steel rails from the Atlantic to the Pacific shore. Between these two populated areas was what was considered to be a vast area of nothingness – a plain inhabited only by the native peoples and by the buffalo which they hunted. Early explorers had crossed this vast space on foot, on horseback or by canoe where stretches of water allowed, but little settlement of any permanent kind took place until the building of the first transcontinental railway line.

Canada's largest ever engineering project, the Canadian Pacific Railway was finished in 1885, linking Montreal in the east with Port Moody and Vancouver in the west. This was a tremendous achievement considering the kind of territory that those who built the railway had to contend with: the muskeg and swamp of the Canadian Shield, the desolation of the vast prairie and the seemingly impenetrable barriers imposed by three sets of mountain ranges in the west. That it was accomplished at all was a tribute, both to its engineers and designers, but also to the labourers who worked long and arduous hours clearing the land and laying track. Many of these workers were Chinese immigrants brought to Canada especially for this task, who endured immense hardship and worked with the ever present reality of being killed on the job – as many of them indeed were.

The construction of the Canadian Pacific Railway created the opportunity to bring settlers from overseas to farm the empty spaces on the prairie. In the process it created the towns and cities which are now parts of the provinces of Manitoba, Saskatchewan and Alberta. After its construction, and for more than 50 years, the Canadian Pacific Railway, and later also the Canadian National Railway, provided the only link between many isolated communities and the rest of the country as many settlements grew up which could only be

The Royal Hudson, a working steam engine, takes tourists up the west coast from Vancouver in British Columbia.

reached by the railway. Many generations of visitors to the country marvelled as the CPR's trains passed through the wilds of the Rogers Pass and looped round the spiral tunnels of the Selkirk Mountains.

The CPR's fastest and most luxurious train was the 'Canadian' which ran daily from coast to coast in both directions, and from whose windows many new arrivals had their first glimpse of the vastness of Canada. For more than 50 years this train and the other transcontinental expresses held the country together, both economically and socially, while the Canadian railway system as a whole provided both the freight and passenger transport that made Canada viable as a country. However, by the middle of the 20th century, with the advent of internal flight and the gradual development of a complex national highway system, the popularity of the railway system had started on a continuous decline, finally reaching the point at which both Canadian National Railway and Canadian Pacific Railway began to lose substantial amounts of money. To prevent the complete collapse of passenger service in many parts of the country, the government eventually agreed to let both companies give up their passenger operations and to hand responsibility for passenger trains over to the government. As a result, although the two large railway companies – and a number of smaller ones – still operate their own freight services and maintain the actual track, all passenger service is now operated by a government subsidiary, VIA Rail. The 'Canadian' still runs – but only three times a week, using the less spectacular northern route through the Yellowhead Pass and not the original CPR track through the spiral tunnels of the Kicking Horse Pass.

VIA Rail

VIA Rail was created by the federal government specifically to bring under one umbrella all passenger rail services in Canada, and thus to increase their efficiency and profitability. Unfortunately VIA has never had a real chance to do this effectively, as the number of passengers travelling by rail has continued to decline ever since its creation. This means that passenger service all through the country has now been pruned to the point at which some communities no longer have access to any passenger train service at all and others have much less than they used to.

For the traveller, these cutbacks to VIA Rail mean that many small communities are no longer accessible by train. Services between the major cities remain intact, however, and the service between the two largest cities in Canada, Montreal and Toronto, although reduced from what it was, still remains quite frequent and efficient. It is also possible to travel from Montreal to all of the maritime provinces, except for Prince Edward Island, which has no rail lines, and Newfoundland, where the famous 'Newfie Bullet', a narrow gauge train that crossed the length of the island, has also been eliminated by the government. Halifax and Fredericton remain served by VIA rail, but the service is neither as frequent nor as fast as it used to be.

However, in spite of all the cutbacks, if time and convenience are not absolute priorities, a trip by rail through part of Canada is still a very scenic and comfortable way to travel. Canadian trains are not the cheapest available form of transport between two places, but they are spacious, well-maintained and have good service facilities both at stations and on board. In fact, crossing any part of the country by train is still one of the best ways to appreciate the diversity of this vast country. There are still a few train trips which allow the traveller to get into some of the country's most scenically beautiful areas. For example, the ride on the Algoma Central Railway from Sault Ste Marie to Hearst, traversing the Agawa Canyon in the Canadian Shield area of the country, is breathtaking – especially in the fall (autumn) when the leaves turn amazing shades of colour along the way. The steam train excursion up the British Columbia coast from Vancouver to Squamish is another worthwhile experience for the train fan, as is the Polar Bear express which travels north from the Ontario town of North Bay to Moosonee, the southernmost town on James Bay, which is still inaccessible by road.

Buying Tickets

Tickets for train travel anywhere in Canada (with some minor exceptions on private lines) can be bought through the computerised system available at any VIA Rail station, and also through most travel agents. Tickets can be bought in advance, and for many trains they must be. For travel of any distance or on very popular train services, it is advisable to make a reservation. VIA Rail's fare structure means that travel is more expensive on the two peak travel days of the week, Fridays and Sundays, with substantial travel discounts being offered for those who travel on the less popular days. As in any other country, trains also tend to be more crowded at holiday times, so that travel around Christmas and in the summer months on scenic routes may need to be planned and booked well in advance. Many of VIA Rail's services also connect with those of Amtrak (American travel by track) in the United States with the result that it is possible to start out from the major Canadian cities and travel well into the United States without having to change trains.

Commuter and Subway Systems

Paradoxically, while main line train service has now been reduced to the point at which it is no longer really attractive to the business traveller, commuter rail services in and out of the major cities have been improved over the last few years and service to the city centres is now quite frequent and efficient from suburban areas. The GO (Government of Ontario) transit service that looks after the needs of commuters into and out of Toronto is run by the provincial government and has an extensive network of lines that reaches all the major suburban communities from which people commute into Toronto. Montreal and Vancouver also have similar commuter networks from their outlying bedroom communities.

Inside the major cities themselves there are also extensive subway networks, and in the case of Toronto, streetcar lines. These urban rail lines are cheap and efficient and operate long hours, making it fairly easy, in conjunction with an extensive network of buses, for people to move from one side of the city to another. One interesting feature of Canadian urban transport systems is that the distance travelled does not relate to the price of the ticket – there is a flat fare regardless of the distance travelled, and if more than one means of transport is used, a transfer ticket can be obtained at no extra cost.

FLYING VISITS

Travelling by air in Canada has replaced the railway for long distance and business travellers. For those travelling out of the country, Canada has nine international airports and two national air carriers to choose from, and these same airports and carriers also provide much of the domestic air service. Canadian Airlines and Air Canada provide scheduled services between all the major cities both in Canada and the

United States and also a regular shuttle service between Toronto, Ottawa and Montreal. To promote business travel on these routes, both of these airlines offer special incentives in the form of rebates and/or free travel privileges to those passengers who use them more than a set number of times during the course of a year.

Outside the major cities, many smaller communities have a municipal airport, served by provincial or local airlines. Some of these are affiliated with the major carriers and others are independent. Where no railway exists, it is usually possible to find some sort of air service between virtually any community of any size in Canada and a major hub, especially in the southern areas of the country. In the northern areas, some form of bush plane service usually serves isolated communities on a regular basis, bringing in supplies and mail as well as passengers. Flying with the smaller airlines, and on the smaller planes that they use, can be an interesting experience for those not used to it. Travellers can rest assured that the government imposes stringent inspection standards to ensure that the safety regulations controlling these planes and their pilots are complied with. Like travelling on the smaller rail lines, flying between the smaller communities – especially in the North – can also be a superb introduction to the splendours of the country and to places not readily accessible by any other means. Even if you need to get to somewhere in the country not served by any regular scheduled service, charter aircraft service is usually available at most small airports – but for quite a hefty price!

THE UBIQUITOUS BUS

Intercity and in-city bus services have been a large part of the Canadian transport scene ever since Canada developed an extensive and efficient highway network, often helping to contribute to the decline of rail travel. Usually cheaper than travel by air or by rail, highway buses run regularly between most of the major centres in Canada and across the country. Companies such as Voyageur and Grey Coach in Ontario and Quebec operate the inter-city services, while the long-distance buses of Canadian Greyhound and its subsidiaries provide inter-provincial service. Most bus companies operate specially-equipped vehicles for very long distances and they will run 24 hours a day so that a trip that involves more than a 12-hour journey will usually continue through the night with the driver of the bus changing periodically, but with the passengers going stoically on to their destination without any delay.

Fortunately, Canadian buses are well adapted to the road conditions and are comfortable and fast. All of them have reclining seats and many now have washroom and refreshment services available. The drivers are meticulously trained, and a bus trip can be quite a relaxing way to travel for those who want to travel between two points in an economical and reasonably speedy fashion. Tickets can usually be purchased in advance at local bus stations for most long trips, and, in fact, this is often a wise thing to do, as buses are occasionally fully booked – especially on Fridays and Sundays and around holiday times. Remember also that buses on which reservations cannot be made often load up on a first-come first-served basis and so the latecomer may be in for an unpleasant surprise!

Bus companies in Canada are either privately or provincially owned and are required to meet stringent safety standards so that their passengers are assured of comfort and efficiency. Many bus companies also provide charter service facilities and/or operate a regular school bus service in their local operating areas, for which they use special buses, in co-operation with the local school board.

THE TWO-CAR FAMILY

One of the reasons why public long distance ground transport services in Canada have been steadily eroded and are not as comprehensive as in many other countries is that most Canadians, like their American cousins, have a long-standing love affair with their cars. Ever since the automobile became easily available and within the budget of the ordinary person, a private car – or even on some occasions two cars

– has been considered a necessity by most Canadians. Cheap gas has contributed to this overwhelming use of cars since the end of World War II, and it is only quite recently that Canadians have begun to reconsider jumping in their cars at any time – even for a trip down to the store on the corner – as the price of gas has begun to creep relentlessly upwards. However, having access to a car remains an important part of the Canadian lifestyle – especially in the country, where there is little or no public transport available.

Like gas, cars are no longer as cheap as they once were. A new car can cost anywhere from C$10,000 and up and up. The competition to sell new cars is fierce and buyers are well advised to shop around carefully for price, options and length of warranty before they settle on which model to buy and what price to pay for it. But even if a new car is not within the budget, there are plenty of used cars on sale in every community. Prices for these are lower than for new cars, although there are some attendant problems that can obviously come with the purchase of a used car. However, the sale of used cars is government controlled so that practices like turning back the odometer are illegal, and most dealers are honest. But care should still be taken when buying a car that appears to be too much of a bargain – as the old saying goes, 'you get what you pay for'.

Car Rental

Leasing and renting cars are also options for those unwilling or unable to put a large sum of money into the purchase of a car. Leasing plans enable the user to rent a car on a long term agreement from the dealer. Leasing a car can often be tax deductible if done through a business, and so is growing in popularity at the moment. Renting a car is generally too expensive for anyone who is interested in getting a car for long term use, but attractive on a casual basis for many people who live in cities with good public transport systems and who only need a car occasionally to make trips that take them out of the city.

Car Maintenance

Maintaining and servicing a car can be done in any number of ways – through the dealer from whom the car was purchased; at one of the many specialist repair shops which can be found in most towns and cities; or even by the owner himself using parts purchased at one of the many retail stores, such as Canadian Tire, which specialise in the automobile business. Canadian winters require some special preparation for the car in the fall – checking the anti-freeze in the radiator and making sure that the tyres are suitable for winter road conditions for instance. Those who are uncertain about what has to be done, or how to do it, will be able to find plenty of garages and automobile care centres where this can be done for a very reasonable charge. Gas can be bought in a similar way as gas stations will often have two kinds of service at the pumps – full serve (where the attendant will do everything for you, including checking your oil and cleaning your windshield) and self-serve where you do everything yourself and then just pay a cashier for what you have bought. The vast majority of cars (and all new ones by law) now use unleaded gas, which is universally available and comes in three kinds – regular (the cheapest), superior and premium. The names of the specific kinds of gas may vary depending on the oil company, but the basic types remain the same. Also, as selling gas is a very competitive business in Canada, the various oil companies usually make their own credit cards easily available to anyone who wishes to buy gas in this way, and often use incentives such as issuing coupons for cheap accessories or free car washes to get people into their stations.

Driving Regulations

Regulations for driving in Canada are determined by each province with the result that some of them do vary from region to region. Specific provincial laws cover areas like the legal driving age, driving tests, vehicle fitness and rules of the road, such as turning, stopping and parking. In fact, the only really accurate way to determine what specifically applies in any given area is to visit an office of that province's Department of Highways and obtain a copy of the provincial Highway Code. However, there is enough similarity between what is allowed in one province and another to make driving throughout the country quite possible for anyone, providing that common sense always prevails. Throughout Canada, all drivers must be licensed by a provincial authority (licences from outside the country are valid only for a specific period of time after arrival and then a Canadian test must be taken) and they must be covered by some form of insurance, which includes protection from at least personal liability and property damage. The cost of car insurance varies from area to area throughout the country and also depends to some extent on your personal driving record.

Roads

Canada boasts a marvellous network of roads, many of which are four-lane or wider. Major highways are scrupulously maintained by the provincial highway departments, whose responsibility also extends to snow clearance in the winter months. Regional and local governments look after the smaller roads, many of which are still gravel surfaced, and can thus be more difficult to navigate, especially in winter. In fact, most Canadian drivers who do a lot of driving on smaller and more isolated roads usually carry basic emergency supplies in the car, in case of a breakdown some distance from a source of immediate help. However, on the whole, travel by car from place to place – whether for a short or long distance – can usually be easily accomplished at any time of year, and in fact, it is not uncommon for people to drive 50 kilometres or more just to go out for dinner or for a medical appointment.

There are several ways of crossing Canada by road, and although to do so takes several days, there are many people who prefer to cross the country this way. Along the major highways, networks of service stations and motel chains have been developed so that long distance

The boat is still very much in use as a means of transport. Canadians love to spend time on boats and on the water.

travellers can usually find somewhere to buy gas or stay the night more or less whenever they wish. During the summer months many Canadians travel long distances on holiday, and motorised camping vehicles are a common sight on the highways all over the country.

TRANSPORT ALTERNATIVES

In addition to the traditional methods of transport, Canada has also developed some which are unique to its particular needs.

With the long coastline and the millions of lakes and rivers, ferry service is a common method of transport. These services range from the major ferries which link Canada's offshore islands, such as Vancouver Island, Prince Edward Island and Newfoundland to the mainland, to small car and passenger ferries across rivers and bays. These are considered to be an integral part of the highway system. During the summer months, other boats of all shapes and sizes can also be seen on practically every lake and waterway throughout the country. These boats range from large excursion craft running public tours for visitors through scenic areas inaccessible in other ways to private craft used both as transport to 'summer homes' often located on islands – or simply as a pleasurable form of recreation.

The land equivalent of the boat is probably the All-Terrain Vehicle (ATV), a kind of four-wheeled dune buggy, whose popularity has grown in recent years and which can often be seen travelling through parts of the country where there are no roads – or where it is more fun not to use the road even if it does exist!

Canada's winter months make the use of boats impractical and different forms of transport emerge to take their place, although ATVs are often used all year round. The snowmobile – a form of motorcycle adapted for use on snow – has become almost as common a form of winter transport as the boat is in summer, while in the northern regions of the country, the sled and dog team can still be found, although its use has become much less common during recent years as the snowmobile has grown in popularity.

– Chapter Eight –

CANADA'S YOUNG AND YOUNG AT HEART

The typical Canadian family is small and usually includes father, mother and two children. There are few extended families. The average family size has dropped from 3.9 persons in 1961 to 3.1 in 1986. This is due mainly to lower fertility rates, but also to an increasing number of single-parent families. The birth rate has declined rapidly. In 1971, the average woman gave birth to 3.2 children. By 1981, that figure was 2.8. Today it is only 1.7.

Family lives have changed dramatically. Social changes, a decline in religious beliefs and liberal divorce laws have resulted in an increasing proportion of marriages that end in divorce. By the mid-

1980s, almost 50% of all marriages ended in divorce. More Canadians are living alone than used to be the case. The number of single-parent families is increasing at a fast rate and in 1986 represented 13% of all families. There has also been a big increase in families with no children at home – either because these are childless families or because the children have left home. However, two-parent families with children are still the norm.

The average age of marriage for men is 27 years and for women 25 years. When speaking of marriage, one can differentiate between marriages that take place in church, civil marriages performed outside church and by a justice of peace, and 'common-law marriages' in which a man and woman live as husband and wife without having been legally married. Increasing numbers of Canadians are living as common-law husbands and wives. In 1986, the number of couples that reported living in such common-law unions represented an increase of 38% over 1981.

CANADA'S YOUNG

As in many other industrialised countries, where both parents are in the workforce, day care for pre-schoolers and children of school age is a major problem. Figures from Statistics Canada show that 68% of women in the full-time workforce have a child under the age of three.

Parents therefore have to resort to the costly solution of sending their children to an assortment of child-minding facilities, such as nursery schools, child minders who will babysit in their own homes or at the child's home, after-school centres, child-minding centres and all-day child care centres. Some of these facilities are funded by the federal or provincial government, but child care is, unfortunately, still very expensive. In order to help such families, the federal government offers tax credits and subsidies. The various provinces may also have different programmes, such as the day care subsidy programme in British Columbia for families with a low income to meet the cost of day care services for their children.

Cheering children show their enthusiasm on Canada Day.

The Block Parent Programme

This is a Canada-wide programme that aims to get each neighbour-hood to protect the children in its area. Quite simply, a Block Parent is a responsible adult who cares about the well-being and safety of children and volunteers his or her home as a refuge for children in distress. After being screened by the police, the Block Parent is given a recognisable red and white sign (that of an adult holding a child by the hand) that he displays in the window of his home where it is clearly visible from the street. A child in trouble – either ill, lost, being bullied, alarmed by strangers or vicious animals, or caught in bad weather conditions – will know he can go to such a house for help. Police are supportive of this programme because it acts as a deterrent to criminals and troublemakers.

The Paper Chase

Constitutionally, education is a provincial matter, that is, education policies are determined by provincial governments and not by the federal government, and so there is a great diversity across the country regarding the primary and secondary school system. Each province has its own department of education and its own system for training teachers. The schools are supported with money derived from local taxes as well as government grants. These schools account for more than 90% of the school population. Canadians enjoy free public education up to end of secondary school, and public schools are non-denominational and open to all.

In all provinces, there are some elementary and secondary schools which are private or independent, and provide an alternative to the public school. These schools are operated by private bodies for specific religious, language, social or educational purposes. They may or may not be denominational, and are all privately funded although some do receive additional financial support from their provincial governments. There are also private kindergartens and nursery schools for children of pre-elementary age.

In five provinces – Newfoundland, Quebec, Ontario, Saskatchewan and Alberta – there are separate schools. These schools are affiliated to certain religious bodies but remain within the public school system. Roman Catholic schools form the largest group. Other separate schools are run by Protestant churches (a combination of Anglican, United Church and Salvation Army) as well as Pentecostal churches and Seventh Day Adventists.

When the children have progressed from day care to school, they are about five or six years old and ready to begin their primary or elementary education, which is general and basic. Elementary school may start with either the kindergarten years or Grade One. They remain in an elementary school until they are about 13 years old, and by that time, they should be in Grade Seven or Eight, depending on the province.

Young children can join a variety of activity groups, such as the Girl Guides.

Children who might have been accustomed to a more regimented school life, having to wear school uniforms and conforming to many rules and regulations concerning colour of shoes, hair accessories, hair length and so on, will be surprised to find that, by contrast, there appears to be a lot of personal freedom in Canadian schools. Except perhaps in some private schools, students are not required to dress uniformly. They attend school wearing their everyday clothes and 'runners' or sport shoes.

Many students who live in rural areas are 'bussed' in to school, while those in even more isolated areas can take their lessons by correspondence.

It is not uncommon for schools to gain and lose students at any time of the year, due to the high mobility of Canadian lifestyle. Many Canadian families relocate from one town to another or change provinces, often as a result of moving to where the jobs are. There are

135

generally few problems enrolling a child in a school. A student is normally accepted into the school nearest the area in which he lives and placed in the standard that is appropriate to his age. Parents should have the child's leaving certificate from his previous school and his latest school report, in order to facilitate enrolment. They can either go directly to the school nearest their new home or to the school board in charge of the area. The child may be required to sit for an assessment paper that will determine which grade he will enter.

The Canadian school year begins in the first week of September and ends in June. There are two weeks of holiday during the Christmas-New Year period, and about 10 days of 'spring break' in March. Canadian students look forward to the months of July and August, during which they enjoy their longest holiday, the 'summer break'. A typical school day begins at 9 a.m. and ends at 3.30 p.m. There is a one-hour lunch break at 12 noon, during which students either have their lunch in school, or at home, if home is near enough.

From Grade Eight or Nine to Grade Twelve, students attend secondary or high school. If one were to compare the Canadian grade system to that of schools following the British educational system, Grade Ten would be equivalent to the General Certificate of Education 'O' level, and Grade Twelve to the GCE 'A' level.

Throughout these years, progress from one grade to another is usually determined by standards set by each individual school. In the junior grades of high school, there is some opportunity for students to select their courses of study according to their interests. This choice is increased at the higher secondary level, when students are offered more subjects, and within the provincial educational requirements, build their own programme from a number of subject areas. In the past, secondary schools were mainly concerned with preparing students for university, and vocational schools were separate, catering to those not going on to a post-secondary education. Today, while there are still technical and commercial high schools, most secondary schools provide a mixture for all types of students. Thus, depending upon resources available, a school may, besides providing the normal and basic academic subjects in the sciences and arts, allow students to study technical subjects such as woodwork, metal-work and auto mechanics; attend commerce courses in business management, data processing and typing; and explore many other possibilities such as home economics, choir and band, peer counselling and tutoring. However, the number and variety of courses is dependent also on enrolment (the number of students who want to take a course) and the availability of a teacher.

After graduation from Grade Twelve, students are either absorbed into the job market, or continue their formal education through community colleges, technical institutes or universities. Those over 15 may leave school and enter the workforce. In Ontario, school is mandatory until the age of 16.

Admission to university usually requires graduation from high school with specific courses and levels of achievement in them. Depending on the university, a general bachelor's degree course in arts or science takes about three to four years to complete, with an extra year for an honours degree. Some faculties leading to the professions, such as law, medicine and engineering, may require the student to have part of or a complete first degree before he can be admitted. The University of Toronto, University of British Columbia and McGill University are three institutions with a well-established international reputation, but there are many other universities in Canada for the graduating secondary school student to choose from. Tuition fees vary according to the institution and the course of study, but a resident of Canada can expect to spend at least C$8000 to C$10,000 a year for tuition, books and other materials and living expenses, and a foreign student at least twice that amount.

Community colleges, institutes of technology, applied arts and sciences, and colleges for training in specific areas such as agricultural technology, fisheries and marine technologies, etc. provide an alternative to a university education. Admission usually requires secondary school graduation. Most college courses, when success-fully completed, furnish the graduate with a diploma or certificate. Some community colleges also offer what are called transfer courses, that is, students taking these courses may after one or two years apply for a transfer into a university where they will complete their course of study. Other colleges may be accredited to one or more universities, so that they may confer on their students taking selected courses a degree from that university.

Education for adults is a rapidly growing area of Canadian education – departments of education, school boards, community colleges and universities may accept mature students who have left secondary school for a number of years and have the necessary academic requirements, and now wish to resume full-time formal education. There are also many part-time programmes and corre-spondence courses for adults who wish to gain credits at various educational levels, or to further their personal interests.

Adolescent Attitudes

Youths from culturally traditional backgrounds who come to Canada for further studies are frequently amazed and even shocked at the manner with which their Canadian friends treat their parents and elders. When visiting friends at home, they may find that the Canadian adolescent does not hesitate to, in the words of one horrified observer, 'scold his parents'.

Perhaps this is because the young Canadian is trained from an early age to voice his thoughts and opinions. Participation is impor-tant in school. When questions are asked, you are expected to respond without having to be called. Children are encouraged to speak up and voice opinions even on 'adult' affairs. For example, young fifth graders may spend some school time listening to the news on the radio and then discuss what they have heard. It is therefore not surprising that if you ask an 11-year-old about an issue that is currently being discussed, you would receive a fairly informed opinion. Students are encouraged to think about and discuss current and controversial matters, and even to write letters to the government giving their opinion on some constitutional matter.

The youth of Canada are used to having their views taken into consideration as views held by future voters, leaders and decision makers. They often find themselves on an almost equal footing with adults around them, parents and teachers included.

Contrast this with the emphasis in a more traditional society on respect for elders and a 'speak only when you are spoken to' standard, and where every elder, whether family or friend, is dutifully greeted with a 'Hello, uncle' or 'Hello, aunt'. A child from such an environment is expected to keep out of adult affairs and concentrate on school work so as to obtain a good grade, get a good job, earn a lot of money and be a success in the world. It is unlikely that an 11-year-old Chinese youth from Singapore, for instance, would be asked for an opinion on political events in the country or world affairs. Coming from a background with such expectations, it is therefore not surprising for a young foreigner or recent immigrant in Canada to suffer from culture shock and to wonder whether a friend who calls everyone, including those much older, by their first names, is not lacking in respect.

Making Friends

Socialising skills are learnt early in life. Schools are often co-educational, with a mix of boys and girls who have every opportunity to learn how to behave with the opposite sex. On Valentine's Day, for instance, an elementary school may host a dance for its students during break time or after school hours, with boys and girls encouraged to mix under the watchful gaze of their teachers. The adolescent begins at an early age to be concerned with such problems as how to be attractive and popular, going to parties, dating and going steady. These worries compete with studies for attention. Sex education is a part of school curriculum. At this time of increased social activity and

139

the pressures of school, the adolescent is particularly susceptible to problems caused by drugs and alcohol. The only solution is for parents to be vigilant and keep a close eye on the kind of company their children are keeping, without meddling in their life of course.

Working Life

Working life is introduced also at an early age. Many children, even when quite young, undertake to do odd jobs to supplement their allowances. They may clean yards, wash cars and windows, or take care of plants and pets when their owners are away. As they grow older, they 'graduate' to delivering newspapers, babysitting, even tutoring, or working part-time at the corner store as a cashier or a delivery person, and earn quite a decent amount of money. This habit of earning money on a part-time basis continues through high school, college and university. For many students, the money earned through a part-time job or a job during the summer often means the difference between being able to pay for the fees for next year's college or university education and having to give it up altogether.

Leaving the Nest

Entering adulthood is a serious business in any community, and this is as true in Canada as anywhere else. Because of the nature of the Canadian educational system and also of the society as a whole, this passage into manhood or womanhood tends to take place when a young person leaves home for the first time. Very often, this is when he or she enters college or university at the age of 18 or 19.

There is no ceremony or special event to mark this transition, but rather, the controlling hand of parents is removed all of a sudden and the young adults finds themselves totally dependent on their own devices, and having to learn the two major survival skills in western society – time and money management.

This means going without transition from the comparative ease of having someone to tell them what time to get up, being nagged (hopefully constructively!) about what to do during the day and how to plan for future events, to suddenly having to organise all this for themselves. This is by no means an easy step! Perhaps even more traumatic is the responsibility for budgeting money. Paying tuition and rent, buying groceries, planning for entertainment, organising travel to and from home – all these adult decisions are suddenly heaped on the young persons who also have to cope with the pressures of being in a totally new social group, removed from the influences of their family and traditional support group.

In many ways, this is just as much a rite of passage as any special ordeal, and it is a very difficult one for many young Canadians to handle. The best preparation for leaving home is for parents to gradually relinquish their control over a year or so before their child is to move away. Let them learn by their own mistakes in a supportive atmosphere before they have to learn the hard way without the benefit of someone close by to pick up the pieces. This isn't easy, however, as many parents live in fear of letting off the brakes too early. But the transition from home to the university or college setting is a fact of life for many children in Canada, and those who are best prepared for it will succeed the best when the inevitable time comes.

A Profile of Canada's Youth

How do we know what Canadian youths are like – their values, concerns, image of themselves, sources of enjoyment and goals? It is to have them speak for themselves, as one study commissioned by the Canadian Youth Foundation has done. In this 1987 study, called 'Canada's Youth Ready for Today', more than 2100 interviews were conducted with youths aged 15 to 24 across the country. Here are some of the results:

• When speaking of their goals, Canadian youth ranked friendship and being loved as tops. Other choices in order of importance were success in what you do, freedom, a rewarding career, a comfortable life and a good education. Popularity was last in the list of 15 goals.

- Friendship and music were cited as the main sources of enjoyment. Relationships with parents and members of the opposite sex were next in importance. Then came television, sports, pets, reading and being by oneself. 'In practice, young people prefer an evening with their friends to being alone. They would rather spend their time listening to music than going to a structured group [activity] led by adults,' observed the study.
- The problems that really bothered the youths, like everyone else, were money and never seeming to have enough time. Life after high school and its unknowns were also important concerns.
- As for smoking, alcohol and drugs, the study revealed that just over a third of Canadian youth smoked cigarettes and drank alcoholic beverages at least once a week. Young men drank alcohol on a more regular basis than women, but they smoked at equal levels. Eighty percent said they never smoked marijuana and 90% said they never used illicit drugs. However, the young people agreed that drugs were readily accessible to those who wanted to try them.

CANADA'S YOUNG AT HEART

Canada is still a country of young people, but its population is aging rapidly. In 1986, the proportion of under-15s was 21%. This is expected to fall to about 16% by the year 2011. The elderly population, on the other hand, is growing more rapidly than any other age group. Those aged 65 and over made up 11% of the population in 1986, and this figure is expected to go up to 16% by 2011.

Most of the elderly (91%) live in private households, while 9% are in nursing homes and other institutions. About a quarter live alone.

How long does a Canadian live? According to 1980–1982 figures by Statistics Canada, the life expectancy of Canadian men is 71.8 years, while that for Canadian women is 78.9 years. In most provinces, the mandatory retirement age is 65 years. But in the provinces of Manitoba, New Brunswick and Quebec, there is no age limit.

A senior citizen enjoys the company of his dogs at a waterfront park.

Thinking Positive

The elderly generally have a very positive image of themselves and don't subscribe to the idea that when you are old, you are over the hill. The word 'old' to describe an elderly person seems almost rude. 'Senior' is the preferred form of reference. In the words of one advertising agency, it's '55 or better' not '55 or older'.

Life is not over; rather, it often takes a new turn. Seniors join choirs, form musical and theatrical groups, go hiking, learn new hobbies, take college and university courses. (Have you ever heard the word 'opsimath'? It means 'someone who learns late in life'!) Bulletin boards in centres catering to the needs of senior citizens, local shops and supermarkets, and the community newspaper are good places to search for news of such activities.

143

A marriage between two seniors is not uncommon. Many widows and widowers seek a new life with another partner, and such weddings are often well attended and blessed by the presence of children and grandchildren.

It often pays to be a senior. Stores offer special discounts on 'Seniors' Day', travel agencies provide cheaper travel, and hunting and fishing licences, camping fees and bus passes cost very much less. Even the income tax department or Revenue Canada recognises the special status of a senior who is 65 'or better' and allows a special deduction from one's taxable income.

Many activities and services are organised for people in this age group. The National Advisory council on Aging delves into matters related to aging and the quality of life for seniors. Canada Post runs a Letter Carriers Alert Programme which ensures that a watchful eye is kept on the homes of seniors and the handicapped. There are homemaker services that help seniors to live independently, offering help with house cleaning, shopping, preparation of meals and personal care.

Retirement Communities

In some parts of Canada, developers have built housing subdivisions especially for seniors, known as retirement communities. These communities are usually close to a small town, maybe near recreational centres, and contain social and recreational facilities like tennis courts, a golf course and a social centre.

Climate is often a major factor when choosing a place to retire to, especially in a country as cold as Canada. Older people who suffer from arthritis, rheumatism, respiratory and other problems feel healthier in warmer climates. In British Columbia, for instance, the beautiful seaside town of Victoria on the island of Vancouver, with its moderate climate, and the sunny Okanagan area in the interior of the province are popular choices for retirement. However, many are lured by the sun down to the United States, into Florida and California.

Is There Life After Retirement?

Recreation when one is a senior must necessarily be something not too physically demanding. Golf, lawn bowling, curling, fishing, gardening and watching television are some that fit the bill. Knitting, quilting, painting and various crafts and hobbies are other interests. In British Columbia, for instance, there is an Annual BC Seniors Games in which active seniors compete in events such as badminton, bagpiping, chess, bridge, cycling, darts, bowling, curling, golf, swimming and track and field.

In summer, the highways are well travelled by those who love the outdoors, and this can be done in a relaxed and not too rigorous way. Many seniors own recreational vehicles (RVs) which are remarkably well equipped, much like a house on wheels complete with bunks, stove, fridge and shower. They spend the summer travelling from

A senior citizen volunteers for an elementary school music class. Many old people remain active after retirement and volunteering is a most worthwhile activity.

145

campsite to campsite all over the country.

If one could, by a large stretch of the imagination, call volunteering a recreational activity, it is without a doubt that senior citizens take on the volunteer's role with gusto. Volunteers are an essential ingredient of Canadian society without whom life would be much poorer. This spirit is nurtured in the young (children go door to door on 'bottle drives', collecting empty bottles and cans to return to the stores for a refund on the deposits, or selling cookies, calendars, etc. to raise funds for various school activities), it is kept alive in adulthood through volunteer work with many service organisations, and certainly carries on into retired life.

Many retired seniors also take on part-time jobs, and retirement can often bring new careers, such as managing apartments or selling real estate; hobbies can become small businesses.

One service of interest with regard to seniors is the Canadian Executive Service Overseas (CESO), headquartered in Toronto, which provides an opportunity for elderly volunteers to use their training, educational background, experience and skills in projects to help in under-developed countries and native communities. The Canadian International Development Agency gives an annual grant to CESO to fund its foreign projects. Retired persons who volunteer are paid travel costs, maintenance and out-of-pocket expenses. These volunteers are usually in the 60- to 70-year age group. They provide technical or management guidance and advice, such as feasibility studies, to manage or guide an established operation and to assist with training.

Moving About

Getting around town can be a task as one gets older, but Canada's seniors are fortunate to be able to take to cycles at that age. Not bicycles, but adult tricycles or trikes. These are what they appear to be – adult versions of the three-wheeled cycle, often with a basket in front for carrying things.

Unfortunately, though, not all seniors are able to get out and about, especially during winter time, when the weather is a major factor in keeping them home. These elderly are commonly referred to as 'shut-ins'. Many towns and cities have volunteer-run organisations that provide essential services to shut-ins, such as 'meals-on-wheels'. The elderly person can, for a nominal fee, have his meals cooked and delivered by volunteers several times a week.

Money Matters

Housing, food, clothing and taxes are the biggest items of expenditure for a retired person. Money matters in particular need to be well planned.

The federal government helps out with Old Age Security pensions and Guaranteed Income Supplements, both of which are tied to the cost of living as measured by the Consumer Price Index.

The Old Age Security pension is paid to a Canadian citizen who is 65 years or older. To get the full pension, you must have lived in Canada for 40 years after the age of 18. A partial pension is available if you have lived here for at least 10 years after age 18. It is not necessary to have paid into this plan or to have worked in Canada.

The Canada Pension Plan is another federal programme that operates in all the provinces but Quebec, where its equivalent is the Quebec Pension Plan. But the senior must first have made contributions to it while he was working before being entitled to draw from it after retirement. The payment is related to how much one has earned and contributed to the plan.

The Guaranteed Income Supplement, based on your income and marital status, and Spouse's Allowance, are geared to the needs of those with a low income. In addition, some provinces have other plans to supplement the income of the elderly who are in financial need, for example, Ontario's Guaranteed Annual Income System.

The Registered Retirement Savings Plan (RRSP) is a private retirement savings plan that supplements federal and company pension programmes. It is a savings plan that is registered with the government so that contributions made to it can be deductible from one's income tax. The amount that is invested and the interest earned from it are not taxed as long as they remain and are not withdrawn from the plan. This is to give Canadians the incentive to save a portion of their income during their earning years to provide income when they are retired.

Any Canadian taxpayer, from any age until the end of the year he or she turns 71, who has earned income – from salaries, bonuses, commissions, business, rental from property – can contribute to an RRSP, which is available through banks, trust companies and investment brokers.

Senior Centres

These have been developed in every province and in the Yukon. They function as drop-in centres, activity centres or multi-purpose centres for older persons. Increasingly, multi-purpose senior centres are becoming focal points for community social services to the aged. They offer a wide range of recreation, cultural and educational activities for older persons to take part in and they provide services of various kinds. These services may include legal aid, help with forms, financial accounting procedures, health counselling, and a housing registry. There may be programmes in which volunteers visit, meals on wheels are delivered, children from schools are encouraged to visit and share their experiences.

Chapter Nine

CANADA AT PLAY

CULTURAL PURSUITS

As has been mentioned earlier in this book, Canadians are often accused of having no culture themselves – at least not one that is distinguishable from the American culture. To some extent this appears to be a valid theory, certainly from a cursory look at the kind of television programmes that are common fare in Canada, or at the kinds of movies that are most popular in the cinemas.

In reality, however, although this might have been true 20 years ago, times have changed and in all aspects of the arts there are signs that a distinctly Canadian culture is becoming identifiable, and this is becoming a lot more assertive than it ever was before.

Canada in Print

Traditionally, Canada's two best-known writers internationally have been the humorist Stephen Leacock, whose *Sunshine Sketches of a Little Town* depicts life as it was in many small communities in Canada in the late 19th century, and the children's writer Lucy Maud Montgomery. Born in Prince Edward Island in 1874, Lucy Maud Montgomery led a lonely childhood, and to pass the time, invented a fictional surrogate, Anne, who lived in a house close to hers with the rather attractive name of Green Gables. Anne was everything that Lucy was not – outgoing, meddlesome and perpetually in trouble, but with a heart of gold when it came to dealing with misfortune, whether hers or other people's. When Lucy Maud Montgomery wrote down the adventures of her fictional friend, they were immediately taken to heart by the Canadian public as a whole, who identified with Anne and were thrilled to be able to read the adventures of a real and likeable Canadian girl, rather than the imported tales of the Americans and the British. Her best-known book, *Anne of Green Gables*, has recently been made into a very successful play which enjoys annual runs at the Charlottetown Festival, and has also been made into a TV movie which draws substantial viewer support wherever it is shown.

Other Canadian writers have also acquired international status in recent years and many of their works have been made into films that have had international distribution. Margaret Laurence's books, *The Stone Angel* and *The Diviners,* have centred on the Canadian experiences with which Laurence was familiar, but have dealt with themes and issues much bigger than national boundaries, while one of Margaret Atwood's latest books, *The Handmaid's Tale*, presents a frightening view of a future which should disturb anyone. In addition to these two literary women, well-known Canadian writers also include Morley Callaghan, Mordecai Richler and W.O. Mitchell. All of these writers write from their own experiences in various parts of Canada, and there is much to be learned from these novels about growing up in Canada – whether on a prairie farm during the

A book about Canada displayed in a shop window. Canadian writing is gaining more popularity and cities like Toronto are important centres for publishing.

Depression or in the Jewish quarter of Montreal in the 50s.

Over the last 20 or 30 years, a surge of popular interest in Canadian writing has stimulated libraries and bookstores to develop specific Canadiana sections, where books both about Canada and by Canadian writers can easily be found. The increase in the quantity and quality of this writing has also led to the foundation of several large exclusively Canadian publishing houses, the most famous of which is probably McLelland and Stewart, publisher of many of the best-known Canadian writers. However, there are now also legions of small publishers, producing not only fiction but everything from self-help books on a wide range of topics (Self-Counsel Press of Vancouver) to complete Canadian encyclopedias (Hurtig Publishing of Calgary). Many of these publishing houses have spent much effort trying to make sure that Canadian writers get the kind of exposure outside the country that they deserve, and slowly – very slowly – Canadian writing has been emerging as distinct and different from American writing.

Canada on Stage

Canadian theatre has also enjoyed the same kind of recent revitalisation experienced by Canadian writing. In fact, it is one of Canada's best-kept secrets that a large number of actors who became famous on the American stage or in the movies were in fact Canadians to begin with. Mary Pickford, Lorne Greene, Christopher Plummer and William Shatner are some big-name actors who have been lured south of the border by the fact that, up to very recently, to make one's name in the theatrical world required exposure either in Great Britain or in the United States. Slowly, that is changing, as theatres become more plentiful in Canadian cities and the Canadian public becomes more attuned to what Canadian playwrights have to say through Canadian actors. Currently, most Canadian cities have small theatres presenting the works of Canadian playwrights on a full-time basis and have developed a loyal and devoted clientele for them.

Strangely enough, however, Canada's best-known theatrical company is dedicated not to the works of a Canadian playwright, but to the works of one of the world's best-known dramatists. The Canadian Shakespeare Festival at Stratford, Ontario, has acquired a reputation for its presentation of Shakespeare that is matched by few other theatrical companies in the world – many people claiming in fact that the Canadian Stratford productions are preferable to those staged by the Royal Shakespeare Company in Shakespeare's own birthplace of Stratford-upon-Avon. Started in a tent by the Irish director Tyrone Guthrie in 1953, the Stratford Festival now has its own custom-built theatre and a season which runs from early April until late November. The Stratford Festival Company has also spawned other festivals celebrating other playwrights in many other parts of Canada, ranging from the Shaw Festival, now an integral part of the scene at Ontario's Niagara-on-the-Lake, to the Robert Service Festival in Dawson City in the Yukon.

In communities without easy access to theatres and concert halls, popular productions are put up by touring theatre companies through arrangements made by local entrepreneurs. Amateur theatrical groups are also a prominent part of most local cultural scenes, presenting works by both Canadian and foreign dramatists, and the standard of their productions is often impressively high.

Tickets for major theatrical performances can be bought through the computerised telephone ticket services, such as Ticketron and TicketMaster, which operate in most major centres, while sources of tickets for local events are usually advertised through local newspapers and radio. Dress for the theatre in Canada is usually casual, although for premieres and special events rather more formal.

Canada on Film

The making and distribution of movies in Canada, not unlike Canadian theatre, was, until a comparatively short time ago, totally dominated by the Americans – with one notable exception. In cinema, in fact, the American cultural stranglehold has proved in many ways a harder grip to break than in other branches of the arts.

So most of the Canadians who wanted to make a name for themselves in the film industry were forced to go south of the border to develop their careers, and the Canadian film industry has remained dominated by the big American studios. Recently, however, partly due to financial encouragement by the Canadian and provincial governments, Canada has become a great place for the shooting of movies on location, and not only in the more scenic parts of the country, such as the Rocky mountains. The city of Toronto, for instance, has been transformed on many occasions into incarnations of various American cities or even into the nameless cites of such films as *Batman* and *Superman*. Without them being aware of it, in fact, many people watching highly publicised feature films all over the world have become familiar with the landscape of the city. The same thing has happened in Montreal and Vancouver, with the result that, although there may still not be many well-known Canadian names among the actors in Canadian films, there are large numbers of well-trained and qualified technicians in the country with expertise on everything from sound recording to the directing of an entire film.

The one notable exception, however, is Canada's National Film Board which has been known worldwide since the 1930s, and its expertise has never really been duplicated anywhere else. The National Film Board was founded just before World War II by a Scotsman named John Grierson, who was brought to Canada for the express purpose of creating an institution whose films would 'interpret Canada to Canadians'.

Beginning initially as a kind of celluloid propaganda machine for the country in the years leading up to and during the war, the NFB has since made many films about the country including some of feature length. However, its directors have become particularly expert in the making of short films, especially those using experimental animation techniques. NFB films have won a large number of Oscars and other film awards for their innovative ideas and their technical excellence, and have given rise to generations of young filmmakers who have gone on to found their own studios and specialise in the making of short high quality films. Some of these studios have come and gone, but there are still a substantial number of young vital film companies in Canada which make award-winning short films. One of the most well known of these companies is Atlantis Films, founded by three young Toronto filmmakers and which is now gaining a reputation as one of the best and most creative studios in the world.

Going to the movies is still a popular pastime in Canada – particularly among young people – and most towns of any size have at least one movie house, showing current releases. Unfortunately, entrance prices to Canadian cinemas have risen steeply over the past few years and are now about C\$7 to C\$8 per admission. However, many cinema chains – which own the majority of Canada's movie houses – offer specially priced admission on specific nights of the week (usually Tuesday or Thursday), and on those nights, it can be quite difficult to get to see popular films!

In most provinces, a classification system determines the age of those who can be admitted to specific movies, with degrees of restricted admission possible. The actual way this system is enforced varies from province to province, but basically it divides movies into those that are 'general' or 'family' in nature to which anyone can be admitted, through various categories such as 'parental guidance' or 'adult accompaniment' where the age at which unaccompanied minors can be admitted is specified, to the restricted film to which no one under 18 can buy a ticket. Advertisements for movies also often carry warnings about the nature of the content – 'violence' or 'graphic language', for instance.

Canadian Home News and Entertainment

Like the film industry, all types of Canadian media have been extremely influenced by the styles of the Americans. Much of the programming on Canadian television is still American in origin and a large number of Canadians who live close to the American border have 24-hour access to American TV stations.

To counter this American influence, the Canadian government set up the Canadian Radio and Television Communications Commission which is now the controlling body for the entire communications industry in the country. The CRTC has laid down very stringent regulations for the content of Canadian radio and television, stipulating that a substantial percentage of the programming has to be of Canadian origin, including music of any kind that is played. Each radio or television station licensed by the Commission is required to file a 'promise of performance' with the Commission outlining the ways in which that station is going to meet the requirements on Canadian content through its proposed kind of programming. The result of these stringently-enforced requirements is that there is now a significantly higher proportion of Canadian content on the air than there used to be and much of it is of very good quality.

Canada's national radio and television service is provided by the Canadian Broadcasting Commission which was originally established as a Crown Corporation in 1936, after a couple of earlier attempts to establish a private national broadcasting network along the American model had failed. The CBC network then comprised only eight broadcasting stations and 16 affiliates, in contrast to the hundreds it now has. Although originally only concerned with the promotion of a national AM radio broadcasting network, over the intervening years, CBC has added a number of other services, including FM and FM Stereo, national and regional television services in both official languages, services to listeners in the far North and multi-lingual services overseas, as well as taking responsibility for broadcasting the proceedings of the federal House of Commons to the nation at large.

CBC is 80% government funded, with the remaining 20% coming from commercial sponsorship and the sale of its programmes overseas. This has unfortunately led to some recent cutbacks in the variety and availability of its regional services, but CBC remains an important cultural link between the diverse regions of the country. Much of its programming is an insightful and thorough examination of current Canadian events. CBC has produced plays and films dealing with practically all Canadian issues, and has dramatised some of the most well-known Canadian classic books including a superlative adaptation of the children's classic *Anne of Green Gables*. News specials on major Canadian concerns have also been dealt with exhaustively by CBC with the result that most Canadians are very well served with information about current issues of concern in their country.

Canadian newspapers have managed to remain much more independent of their American counterparts than other segments of the media. Due to its vast size, Canada has not really developed a truly national newspaper, but rather a series of large regional ones. The country's biggest newspaper, *The Globe and Mail*, is Toronto-based but comes the closest to being a national newspaper, while other newspapers such as the *Vancouver Sun*, the *Toronto Star* and the *Montreal Gazette* deal largely with both international and regional news for subscribers in their own areas. Local newspapers can also be found in many small towns throughout the country, often coming out weekly and dealing with events of interest to the surrounding community. Curiously enough, unlike other forms of media, American publications have never really caught on, and although papers like *USA Today* are readily available on the streets of Canada's large cities, they have never enjoyed the success which their electronic counterparts have done with Canadians.

Conversely, the Canadian magazine market does defer largely to the Americans – both *Time* and *Newsweek* enjoy a large circulation in the country and are read by many Canadians. However, Canada does have its own news magazine, named *Macleans*, which enjoys a large and dedicated subscriber list. In other areas of magazine publication, although American magazines are readily available, there has also been a steady growth of Canadian-based magazines dealing with matters of interest from computers to the environment.

Canadian Art

The Canadian art world was for a long time dominated by the scenic painter. The works of Paul Kane, who first depicted the Canadian wilderness in the 19th century, still give to modern Canadians a sense of the visual history of the country, while Canada's most famous landscape artists, collectively known as the Group of Seven, dedicated their lives to depicting the Canadian countryside – especially that around the area of the Canadian Shield.

The Group of Seven was formed in 1911 by seven Canadian painters, all of whom were thrilled by the potential of the Canadian landscape as artistic material, and wanted to investigate through their

A street artist making sketches while passers-by pause to look.

work, the relationship between nature and art. Franklin Carmichael, Lawren Harris, A.Y. Jackson, Franz Johnson, Arthur Lismer, J.E.H. MacDonald, F.H. Varley and Tom Thompson were the original members of the group to which A.J. Casson was added in 1926 and Edwin Holgate of Montreal and L.L. Fitzgerald of Winnipeg at a later date. Their paintings are a celebration of the wildness of Canada and of its colours as the seasons change, and many of them have now become collector's items. Although the Group of Seven was disbanded in 1933, their influence on Canadian painting has remained very strong, and artists in other parts of the country, such as Emily Carr in British Columbia, have followed in their tradition, with the result that the scenic splendour of Canada is well represented in Canadian painting.

The contemporary Canadian art scene is much more varied, and modern Canadian artists work in a number of different media and styles. The influence of the natural beauty of the country is still strong, however, and native art work, particularly that of the Inuit people of the North, has become very popular and influential. The works of the major native artists, such as the west coast's Bill Reid, are in great demand among collectors and have led to a renewed interest in the folk roots of Canadian art. As a result, many modern Canadian artists are now experimenting with traditional folk art styles and incorporating them into contemporary works, leading to a peculiarly Canadian blend of homegrown tradition and modern international art influences.

To display the works of Canadian artists, both public and private art galleries have proliferated over the last 10 to 15 years. Practically every city in Canada now has some form of art gallery and/or art society which present regular collections of the work of both nationally known and local artists. The federal government's Art Bank, which purchases and distributes Canadian paintings all over the country for exhibition in federal buildings, has done much to bring an awareness of the art scene to every Canadian. During the summer months, much local art is also displayed at outdoor exhibitions, where those interested in art can purchase good contemporary pieces.

OUR SPORTING SELVES
The Great Canadian Sport

There can be no doubt that if there is a national sporting obsession in Canada, it is with the game of hockey. A careful distinction has to be made here, however, for what a Canadian would call hockey does not refer to the game played on a conventional outdoor field – this is somewhat derisively known as field or ground hockey – but rather to the great Canadian-invented game of ice hockey. Most Canadian males grow up playing hockey on frozen ponds and streams during winter and many of these boys become starry-eyed at the thought of becoming a member of one of the NHL (National Hockey League) teams whose members are now among the highest paid sportsmen in the world.

As ice hockey is undoubtedly the great Canadian sport, the hockey player is naturally one of Canada's most enduring heroes. Current National Hockey League players are paid extremely large salaries to play a game that is second nature to all Canadian small boys while famous hockey players of the past are celebrated in their own Hall of Fame. Among the members of the Hockey Hall of Fame are such people as Bobby Orr (inducted 1979), Bobby Hull (inducted 1983) and 'Rocket' Maurice Richard (inducted 1961). The current hockey superstar, Canadian born and bred and widely regarded as one of the all-time greats, is Wayne Gretzky, who plays for the Los Angeles Kings. The NHL includes both Canadian and American players, but most of the well-known players for all the major teams – which include the Toronto Maple Leafs, the Los Angeles Kings, the Edmonton Oilers and the New York Rangers – are Canadian in origin, just as the reverse is true in the great American sport of baseball. Many players past and present are household names and their pictures appear on a vast variety of memorabilia ranging from T-shirts and

caps to hockey cards, which are regularly traded among fans of the game. In fact some of the rarer hockey cards can reach collector prices as high as several thousand dollars if they represent an all-time great player.

Watching a hockey game is almost a ritual experience for many Canadians whose Saturday nights are dedicated to the hockey game on television or in the local arena. There are various levels of hockey available both to players and spectators and there is a vigorous selection procedure for those youngsters who wish to make it up the ladder of playing expertise. Many Canadian parents in all parts of the country rise every day early in the morning to take their offspring to hockey practice because the sport is so popular that it is hard to find a time when the local ice surface is not being used for practice.

Other Lesser Sports
While there is no doubt that hockey is the sport of choice in Canada,

other international sports are commonly played in Canada. Among these are baseball, tennis, basketball, squash and lacrosse (which is in origin itself Canadian). Initiation into these sports begins early for young Canadians as their fundamentals are widely taught in all school systems during Physical Education classes. All of them are also played in a strong league structure across the country, and for some sports, also in competition with American leagues. Canada is also represented at the Olympic Games and the Commonwealth Games, where it has in recent years become particularly noted for its track and field athletes.

Outdoor Sports

Canadians are great outdoorsmen. With such a large country and so much of it still wilderness, it is scarcely surprising that all kinds of sports which encourage people to take to the countryside are extremely popular.

Canoeing is universally popular throughout the country, with many of the large national and provincial parks offering facilities for both the experienced and the novice paddler. Canoes and lessons for the inexperienced can be purchased in most major centres, and certainly travelling in this way is one of the most attractive ways to see the Canadian wilderness.

Two other very popular ways of getting involved with the Canadian wilderness are winter sports that are well represented throughout Canada. For the less energetic, snowmobiling is one way of travelling through the Canadian countryside, although it is inevitably accompanied by the din of motor noise and the smell of gas. For the pure at heart, there is always cross-country skiing, a sport that has been growing in popularity over the last few years with the development of the environmental movement. As with canoeing, there are a large number of trails all over the country set up for those who wish to use skis – many of which are closed to snowmobilers who have their own trails in other places.

Canadians learn to ski at a young age. As snow covers the whole country in winter, skiing is a favourite Canadian winter sport.

For the ski purists, facilities for downhill skiing abound – in the western Rockies one finds downhill skiing to challenge even the most intrepid skier, such as the runs at Whistler and Blackcomb north of Vancouver, but there are also fine downhill ski runs in the east, especially in the Laurentian mountains above Montreal and in the Muskoka region north of Toronto. In fact, wherever one lives in the country – except on the vast flatness of the prairies – skiing facilities (both cross-country and downhill) are usually not far away, often within an hour's drive of home.

Hunting and fishing are also popular summer and fall sports. With its many lakes and great expanses of wilderness, Canada is a hunter's and fisherman's paradise. There are strictly enforced seasons for most species, however, and catches are limited by law. Those wishing to hunt deer and/or moose with a firearm must take a special hunter safety course before setting out – and penalties are quite severe for those who do not.

Like most avid outdoorsmen, Canadians are great campers and many camping sites can be found in all areas of the country. The tent

has now been supplemented with the convenience of the tent trailer or the mobile home – the difference being in the cost of the equipment and the comparative luxury which they offer. But whatever the camper chooses to drive around in, a vast variety of camp sites are available for his use – and very inexpensively in most cases! The majority of sites now have shower and toilet facilities, and quite a few of them have special hook-ups for power and water for those who travel in more comfort.

Many of the most scenic areas in all parts of the vast Canadian outdoors have been set aside as protected parkland for the permanent enjoyment of their visitors. In fact, as soon as the transcontinental railway was completed in 1885, bringing with it the beginning of tourism to the most scenic spots in Canada, it was realised that many of these areas would need protection if they were to be kept in their natural scenic condition. As a result, in November 1885, Banff Hot Springs was the first to be designated a National Park, and from this beginning came today's extensive National Park system. In 1964, a National Park policy was formulated and national parks were divided into several regions and types, from those in the High Arctic to the Pacific Rim National Park, from Point Pelee Bird Sanctuary to the Fundy National Park on Canada's east coast. These parks are now managed by Parks Canada which is a department of the federal government, and any type of development within these areas is strictly controlled.

Provincial governments have also developed a similar network of parks, ranging from those protecting and conserving resources to those developed to allow the citizens of a particular province to see its scenic variety for themselves. Information on these parks – including which ones contain camping facilities – can be obtained through the various provincial Ministries of Tourism, which also maintain information centres during the summer months at strategic locations throughout the province – in shopping malls, highway service centres and at major scenic and historical attractions.

CANADIAN WILDLIFE

One of the joys of being in the Canadian outdoors is the contact with Canada's abundant wildlife. Animals from the large moose, bear and caribou to the smaller fox, beaver and groundhog and the tiny chipmunk can be found in most parts of Canada – although most of them are best admired from a distance, as direct contact with some will frighten them badly and can even be quite dangerous on occasion! Canada is also home to a large number of species of bird – ranging from the large eagle and hawk to the tiny hummingbird.

Moose and bear are the largest species of Canadian wildlife and are often found in abundance in the north. Moose – which look like a larger version of the deer – are usually quite bashful and non-aggressive (unless they are in heat or with young), although they can be a menace if they wander onto the roads at night. There are three species of bear in Canada – polar, grizzly and black/brown bear. The

The grizzly bear is an endangered species. This young bear was photographed at the Metro Toronto Zoo.

polar bear is found only on the arctic coasts and islands, and although usually quite easy to spot, must be approached with extreme caution, while the grizzly, large and often dangerous, is restricted to the north and west of the country, especially in mountainous areas. Black or brown bears can be found almost anywhere – and often make a nuisance of themselves in small communities and campgrounds by trying to get into unattended food or garbage.

The beaver is the symbol of Canada and lives almost everywhere in Canadian swamps and wetlands. Beavers are nocturnal animals, however, and so are not always easy to spot, as they tend to remain in their specially constructed houses during the day. Beavers can often cause great damage to wooded areas and crops, due to their annoying habit of using their strong front teeth to cut things down for their own use. Other small mammals like the groundhog and chipmunk are equally abundant, and easier to find – the latter will even sometimes come and take food from your hand.

Two Canadian birds also deserve special mention – the Canada goose and the loon. Both of these birds are migratory and can usually only be seen during the summer months on ponds and lakes all over the country but especially in the Canadian Shield. In the spring and fall, the migration of the Canada goose is considered to be one of the signs of seasonal change.

INDOOR PURSUITS

Not all Canadians are outdoorsmen – at least not all the time – and there are many indoor pursuits which are equally popular in the country. These can range from collecting – a passion with many of those people who haunt flea markets and auctions on the weekends – to model railroading and card playing. Hobby shops, found in all urban centres, cater to all kinds of interests and there are a number of clubs and associations in all regions of the country which devotees of a particular pursuit can join to practise and/or learn whatever skill or pastime it is that takes their fancy.

Canadians also have a great and enduring interest in all kinds of crafts – from appliqué to quilting and weaving – with a tremendous variety in between. For the newcomer interested in a particular skill, finding a teacher is usually not difficult, for many of them are, in fact, taught through night school classes, sponsored by local educational organisations. The products of local craftsmen are regularly displayed at craft shows and exhibitions – especially during the summer months – where many examples of extremely fine workmanship can be purchased quite inexpensively, while many areas also have small, privately operated craft shops which are often run by local art collectives and are open all year round.

If indulging in a private passion or acquiring a specific skill is not one's idea of an indoor sport, there are even some common pursuits which combine the sporting instincts of Canadians with the desire to participate in some kind of social experience. One of the most popular indoor pastimes in Canada is probably the game of bingo, and bingo halls are common sights in every community of any size (see *The Canadian Mosaic*). Bridge and curling are also popular indoor pursuits and facilities for both of these are equally common. Perhaps the most common indoor pursuit of all, however, in recent years has become the viewing of home videos, and the growth of businesses renting these to customers for one or two nights has been phenomenal.

– Chapter Ten –

THE SOCIAL LIFE

FOOD

'The basic Canadian meal is meat and potatoes plus other vegetables.
Eggs, cheese and fish are common meat substitutes, while spaghetti,
noodles and rice or beans are a few common substitutes for potatoes.
Vegetables and fruit are included in most meals. Generally speaking,
Canadians do not spice their food heavily.'

– from the admissions handbook 1990/91 of the University of
Victoria, British Columbia, giving students an idea of what to
expect in Canadian food.

170

Is there any such thing as Canadian cuisine? Canadian food is hard to define. It varies tremendously across Canada, especially since each ethnic group has brought to its new country the tastes of its people. Canadian food is therefore French in Quebec, British in most parts of Canada. In the cities, you will find Jewish, Chinese, Italian, Indian and other cuisines. Chinese food is especially easy to find. Even in small towns, cafés and restaurants offer 'Canadian and Chinese smorgasbord', that is, a western-Chinese assortment of food sold buffet style, although this seems to be more common in the west than the east. *Chow mein* (fried noodles), sweet and sour pork and *wonton* (meat dumplings) soup are standard offerings.

Canadian Smorgasbord

Some may argue that there is no Canadian cuisine in the same way as there is Chinese, Indian, French or Italian cuisine, but over the years, immigrants have brought many ethnic foods with them that have now become associated with those areas of Canada where they settled.

There are also some foods that are native to the country, for example, Saskatoon berries, maple syrup (which is also produced in the northeastern American states), fiddleheads and Arctic char.

It must also be mentioned that, as with many other things, there are some foods such as corn on the cob, clam chowder, baked beans, sourdough bread and pancakes that are as much Canadian as American, whether this fact is well known or not.

Certainly, there are many regional delicacies to explore. Here is a sampling of some of them:

- In **Newfoundland,** hunting for seals for their fur and oil has resulted in a culinary by-product, flipper pie, made from the flippers of young harp seals. Many organisations hold flipper pie suppers during April and May. Fish, especially cod, is available all year round, fresh, dried or salted. It is so plentiful that finding sufficient cod tongues for a recipe is no problem in this province. Cod tongues apparently have a delicate flavour and a texture much like that of scallops or clams. Fried in batter, cod tongues can be served as an appetizer or for breakfast or brunch.

- **Nova Scotia** has a varied cuisine brought by Scottish, English, French and German settlers. Try Solomon Grundy, a traditional Mennonite recipe of salted herring pickled with vinegar, sugar and spices. Or Acadian blueberry grunt, in which spoonfuls of a soft dough mixture are cooked in a hot blueberry sauce.

- **New Brunswick** is known for its clam chowder, a rich, thick broth that has New Brunswickers ecstatic when it is made with large clams from the Shediac area.

  When in the province, look also for a distinctive vegetable called fiddlehead that is really the young curled shoot of the Ostrich Fern. While it grows all along the east coast of North America, from as far south as Virginia to New Brunswick and a little way inland, not many places have embraced it as a culinary delight. However, in New Brunswick, it is gathered from the woods in the spring almost as soon as it pokes its head above the soil. It is not very well known in western Canada, where supermarkets have to introduce it to their customers. Recipe books recommend that fiddleheads should be lightly boiled and served buttered and seasoned, or with Hollandaise sauce.

  Another 'vegetable' that is associated with New Brunswick is an edible seaweed, called dulse. It is harvested in the summer time from Grand Manan Island, where it grows on the rocks.

- **Prince Edward Island** is well known for its potatoes, the main product of its farmlands, as well as seafood – oysters from Malpeque Bay make oyster bisque, a kind of rich soup, while plentiful fresh lobsters can be steamed, boiled, added to salads or prepared into delicious lobster Thermidor.

- **Quebec** has given to Canadian cuisine *tourtiere*, pea soup, maple syrup and Oka cheese. *Tourtiere* is a French-Canadian meat pie. It is traditionally made with pork and served on Christmas Eve after midnight Mass. There are many cheeses made in monasteries in Quebec. Oka is one that is well known, a soft and highly flavoured cheese made by the Trappist monks.

Special mention must be made of maple syrup, which is harvested or 'sugared off' in the early spring in the east – in both Quebec and Ontario – where most of Canada's maple syrup is produced. Spring is the only time because that is when the days are warm and the nights still cold – it is the signal for sap of the tree to move up from the roots to the tree. Mature maple trees are tapped by driving a spigot into the side of the tree. A bucket or plastic tube attached to the spigot collects the sap. The sap is sweet but thin. To make a gallon of syrup, you would have to collect about 40 times the amount of sap, place it in special containers and boil it down until the syrup is of the right consistency.

'Sugaring off' is a great social event. Everybody in the village and on the farms gathers for this. It is a time the kids love, when they can enjoy 'sugar on snow' – chewy bits of maple syrup toffee which is made by just splashing some of the hot, thick syrup onto the clean snow still on the ground. The snow cools the syrup into toffee which you can then pick up and sink your teeth into.

- **Ontario** cuisine has a rich heritage to draw from – Mennonite settlers brought *schmier kase*, a buttermilk curd, and smoked sausage, while British Loyalist settlers preserved such English recipes as creamed kippers and minced lamb pie. In fact, in recent years, the presence of ethnic communities from all over the world has made both the cooking ingredients and prepared food available in Ontario extremely varied, especially in Toronto.

- When in **Manitoba,** try the Winnipeg goldeye, a small herring-like fish that is smoked over oak logs and then dyed a deep coral red. Ukrainian settlers have contributed the *pirozhki*, a meat pie appetizer.

- **Saskatchewan** has many native wild berries, of which the Saskatoon berry is perhaps the most well known, and many migratory birds that could end up on the dinner table, such as the

173

During the early spring, maple syrup is collected in buckets such as these.

partridge and prairie chicken. The Saskatoon looks like a blueberry, and is often made into a Saskatoon berry pie. Having a corn roast is a popular pastime. With the husks pulled back and the silks removed, freshly picked corn (it should be eaten almost immediately after being picked as the natural sugar in the corn turns to starch as time goes on) is soaked in water, cob and all, for about half an hour to ensure that the husks are wet through. It is then drained and brushed with melted butter, husks put back in place, and covered with aluminium foil and placed over the glowing coals of a bonfire. After 20–30 minutes, the corn is ready for eating.

- **Albertans** are proud of their cattle which they believe produces the best beef steaks. An unusual beef dish is Chuck Wagon Stew, a reminder of days when the covered wagon used to bring dinner to cowboys on the range.

A beef barbecue Canadian style.

THE SOCIAL LIFE

- **British Columbia** is noted for its salmon, of which there are five varieties – chum, coho, pink, sockeye and spring. From the tiny Saltspring Island, off the coast of Vancouver, comes tender Saltspring lamb, best roasted and eaten with fresh mint sauce.
- Game food must certainly be mentioned when thinking of the **Yukon and Northwest Territories,** for it still forms a large part of the local diet. When in the North, you might have an opportunity to try moose roast (but the meat must be marinated for as long as one to two days to counteract its gamey flavour) and buffalo stew. Pemmican, a mixture of pounded buffalo meat and berries, no longer finds its way onto the dinner table but it used to be a staple of the early explorers. And any discussion of food in the North is never complete without mention of sealskin boots, which Inuit women actually chew upon to soften them before use. In 1909, the Bishop of Yukon, Isaac O. Stringer, and his companion were lost but survived the ordeal by eating their sealskin boots, toasted and boiled!

A Typical Canadian Menu

Having been briefly acquainted with the tremendous variety that makes up Canadian cuisine, the reader might like to try **An all-Canadian dinner menu** as described by Pierre and Janet Berton, in *The Centennial Food Guide, A Century of Good Eating*:

Oysters Canadian
Pea soup
Brome Lake duckling with wild rice dressing
Fiddleheads
Young PEI (Prince Edward Island) potatoes
Mashed pumpkin
Blueberry whip with lemon
Oka cheese
Coffee

• **Oysters Canadian**: chop very fine, $1/4$ cup each lamb's quarters (pigweed); fresh young dandelion greens; romaine lettuce; fresh celery leaves and curly endive plus 4 sprigs fresh parsley and 2 large fresh green onions, tops included. Add: 2 strips lean bacon, fried crisp, cooled and well crumbled; 1 tsp anchovy paste; 1 tsp tarragon; 1 tsp dry English mustard; $1/2$ tsp chervil; 4 fennel seeds, well crushed; 1 tbsp fresh chives, well chopped; 1 tbsp onion juice; 1 tsp lemon juice; $1/2$ cup bread crumbs; $1/4$ cup grated cheese; a dash of Worcestershire sauce, Tabasco sauce and Angostura bitters; salt and ground fresh pepper to taste.

Pound the whole in a mortar to the consistency of a paste, blend with $1/4$ cup creamed butter slowly in a blender.

Open on the half shell one dozen Malpeque oysters and cover each with the mixture. Top with grated cheese. Broil on a pan of wet heated rock salt for 10 minutes.

• **French Canadian pea soup**: Soak 1 cup split peas, yellow or green, in cold water overnight. Drain. Put in a pot with a ham bone to which some meat is still clinging, together with 2 chopped onions; 2 chopped carrots; 4 stalks chopped celery; 5 peppercorns; 1 bay leaf; a little salt; Worcestershire sauce and monosodium glutamate. Simmer for several hours or overnight until the peas and vegetables are all one smooth puree. Serve with crisp, crumbled bacon.

• **Brome Lake duckling with wild rice dressing**: Place 1 cup wild rice and $1 1/2$ tsp salt in 5 cups chicken stock and bring to the boil slowly, stirring to prevent sticking. Then cook without stirring for about 45 minutes until tender. Drain and add 1 tsp celery salt; 1 tsp thyme; 1 tsp sage; $1/2$ onion, chopped; 1 stalk celery, chopped; 1 cup sliced sautéed mushrooms; salt, pepper and butter to taste. Fill ducks lightly with rice, add $1/2$ orange per duck and baste while roasting with red wine and orange juice.

(The Bertons do not give any recipe for fiddleheads and young PEI potatoes, but the fiddleheads may simply be boiled very quickly over high heat and seasoned to taste and the potatoes roasted.)

- **Mashed pumpkin**: Cook the pulp of one pumpkin until tender and mash together with $1/2$ tsp dill; 1 tsp cracked pepper; $1/2$ chopped onion and $1/2$ cup sour cream.
- **Blueberry whip**: Soak 1 tbsp gelatine in $1/4$ cup cold water. Dissolve in $1/4$ cup boiling water. Mix the grated rind of 1 lemon in $3/4$ cup sugar. Dissolve sugar in boiling water and gelatine. Add 3 tbsp lemon juice; 1 cup lightly crushed blueberries; 1 tbsp Cointreau. Chill until partly stiff and then beat until frothy. Whip 4 egg whites with $1/3$ tsp salt and whip into the gelatine and blueberry mixture until it holds its shape. Set in a wet mould and serve with Cointreau-flavoured whipped cream.

Shopping for Food

This is most commonly done in supermarkets, which have the standard offerings found in supermarkets everywhere. Meat and vegetable counters are well stocked, but the same cannot be said for fresh seafood. Unless you live along the coast, the selection of fresh fish and other seafood is poor. Cod, trout, mackerel, halibut, salmon and snapper can usually be found. Prawns and shrimp are often sold in cooked or frozen form. Live crabs are hard to find and therefore expensive. Instead, there is crab meat of the artificial kind. Fresh mussels, clams and oysters are also scarce, and when there is squid, it is often bought by fishermen for bait.

Sometimes there are speciality sections that cater to the needs of a large minority population. So, even in a small store, there might be Chinese, Japanese or Indian spices and condiments if there is a sizeable Chinese, Japanese or Indian population. Moreover, with the current health food trend, soyabean products are a familiar sight on the shelves. Western taste buds are more educated now when it comes to Asian, especially Chinese, cuisine. So soya sauce can be found next to tomato ketchup, bean sprouts and Chinese cabbage (known as *bok choy*) to alfalfa sprouts and broccoli, and soyabean (called *tofu*) products range from the curd and milk to burgers and cheese.

Pick of the Crop

As in many other countries that have large agricultural areas, journeying through farm country in the summer or autumn often provides the traveller with an opportunity to stop by fruit and vegetable stands along the secondary roads. It is both a delight and a relief from long and tiring car journeys to pause and buy freshly picked fruit and vegetables of the season, such as corn, melons, apples, cherries and strawberries, etc. A variation of this is the numerous farms where you can pick your own fruit. These farms often advertise with 'pick-your-own' signs along the road. The whole family is encouraged to get out there and enjoy picking the fruit, and there is great satisfaction in knowing that you have truly 'farm fresh' produce. You can also eat a few berries as you pop your harvest into your containers, but it is good etiquette not to eat more than you collect.

Canadian Cheer

Canada produces its own wine and beer. The brewing industry in Canada has long been dominated by the large national beer manufacturers, whose products have become in some ways an indispensable part of Canadian culture. Such beers as Molson's Canadian and Labatt's Blue are available coast to coast and are enjoyed by millions of Canadians, who love their beer served cold. There are also a number of small local breweries, called 'micro breweries', whose products, although not so widely available as those of their giant competitors, are increasingly catching on with connoisseurs of fine beers. Many of the small breweries base their brewing procedures on European models, manufacturing their beers without additives and following traditional guidelines to preserve the character of their products. Some of these guidelines are as old as the German Bavarian Purity Act of 1516.

Such local beers are usually available through the beer retailing outlets in each province, and are also increasingly being sold in special local 'brew-pubs' whose clientele dedicate themselves to the sampling of beer which is different from the conventional.

Canadian wine is generally the cheapest one can get here, costing about C$5–$6 for a 750 ml bottle. The main wine-making regions are British Columbia's Okanagan Valley and Ontario's Niagara region.

Canadian whisky is made with rye, and so is known as rye whisky. Two leading Canadian brands are Seagram's V.O. and Hiram Walker's Canadian Club Whiskey.

Liquor licensing laws vary from province to province, but alcoholic drinks are generally available only from government liquor stores and licensed wine and beer stores, and not from the local corner store or supermarket, except in Quebec. The legal drinking age varies according to province too, but is either 18 or 19 years.

Dining Out

In Canada this can be an experience ranging from the mundane to the exotic. Small café-restaurants offer inexpensive lunch and dinner buffets or smorgasbord meals as well as a la carte selections. A decent meal can be had for about C$6 to C$12. Franchise establishments, which range from the all-familiar A&W and McDonald's hamburger restaurants to regional chains, for example, Whitespot and ABC restaurants in the west, offer a comparably-priced menu. Naturally, given Canada's immigrant history, there are many small speciality places that cater to ethnic tastebuds and the adventurous epicurean, and expensive restaurants where one undoubtedly pays not only for the food, but also the quality of ambience and service.

Unlike in some countries, such as Australia, the practice of bringing your own wine or liquor to the restaurant (BYO or 'bring your own') is not a common or accepted one here.

As for portions one can expect, this is really a subjective matter, but if one had to generalise, it would not be wrong to say that Canadians are big eaters and you can therefore expect portions to be very generous.

There is no automatic service charge, so tipping is necessary and can be hard to remember if you are used to having a service charge included in the bill. In Canada, a charge for service is added to your bill only if you consent to it. If you are unsure of what to do, most tourist guide books recommend that you leave anything from 10 to 20% of the total bill.

Pot Luck

This is an easy and popular way for organisations to hold social gatherings without the headaches that accompany feeding the hungry. Each family that attends brings something to contribute to the common table. If you are invited to a pot luck supper, it is a good rule of thumb to bring enough to feed your own family. You should be responsible for what you bring – reheating the food, refrigerating and serving, and taking home your pots and utensils when you leave. If it is an unusual cuisine that you are offering, make sure you let your hostess know so that guests can be warned if a dish is particularly hot and spicy, or if it contains unfamiliar ingredients. A pot luck function, therefore, can be a great adventure and it usually works out such that there is a great abundance and variety of food to enjoy.

The Perfect Guest

It is difficult to decide what you should bring when going to a friend's for a meal. It seems to be just as much a Canadian custom as it is an Asian one not to arrive empty-handed, but what should one bring? It is best to play this by ear. If you know your host fairly well, you might offer to bring something for the table, a dessert perhaps. Canadians are often clever at preserving and pickling, and a jar of home-made jam often makes a perfect gift. A bottle of wine, if your host drinks, or a box of chocolates are safe bets. If you have a well-established garden, some blooms that are in season will also do.

When you arrive at your host's, do you take off your shoes or keep them on? There is no established custom regarding this. Rather, it depends upon personal preference. Some Canadians do and some don't. A friend said he found the habit more prevalent in the west than in the east, while another said city folk did not, but country folk did, on account of the fact that their shoes might be dirty from working on the farm! Most homes have wall-to-wall carpeting. Your host or hostess might not wish to have the carpets muddied. So again, one should play this by ear. A quick glance around the entrance will tell you what is expected.

If a Canadian friend invites you to spend a weekend at home with his family, you will want to make a good impression. A good guest is one who does his best not to disrupt the normal functioning of the household, so you should find out when meal times are, at what time the family gets up in the morning, and at what time they go to bed. An offer of help from you when you see your host and hostess working in the kitchen or garden, for example, may be declined but will always be appreciated. After you have returned home, remember to send a thank-you card or letter for the hospitality that you have received.

THE VOLUNTEER SPIRIT

'Be a local hero' is the slogan of a public awareness programme across Canada that seeks to encourage a spirit of philanthropy among Canadians young and old. Certainly, the volunteer spirit is strong in Canadian society, probably because it is nurtured in Canadians from an early age. Schools play an important role. For instance, during Forestry Week, teachers take their charges out into the forests to plant seedlings, and on Earth Day or Environment Week, there are excursions into the countryside to pick up garbage. Schools often hold fund-raising projects, and children and parents are expected to rally round and volunteer help during their free time to hold bake sales, garage sales, organise concerts and other activities. Many organisations and community services depend on volunteers to function – for example, Boy Scouts and Girl Guides leaders are often parents who volunteer their time after work so that their children are able to participate in these activities; similarly, the swim club, gymnastics club, baseball and hockey teams, too, depend on volunteers who are interested in providing these activities in their area. Services for the sick, elderly and handicapped and fund-raising for various charitable organisations are other areas where volunteers are needed – to deliver meals to the elderly who are house-bound (called 'meals on wheels'), to take the tea wagon around hospital wards and to visit the sick, to go door to door around the neighbourhood canvassing for numerous charities.

The 'Bee'

The 'bee' is a prime example of Canadian community spirit. 'Bees' began during pioneer days in Upper Canada when whole communities would get together to perform a service for one of their members or to make some contribution to the progress of the entire community. Modelled on the swarming behaviour of the honey bee, this coming together of neighbours and friends still survives in rural communities today, if there is a large project which needs extra manpower to complete or if someone suffers a disaster and needs the help of the community.

Originally, there were all kinds of occasions which called for a 'bee' – from erecting farm buildings and harvesting (the most common) to logging, stumping (the removal of tree stumps) and the butchering of livestock.

Farmers' wives often held quilting, preserving or knitting 'bees' at the same time as their menfolk were outside at work on another project. And when the work was done, a huge meal would be served and the evening hours spent socialising.

In his book *Pioneer Days in Upper Canada*, Edwin Guillet quotes a contemporary observer as commenting that 'after the specific duties of the "bee" were ended, the young men indulged in trials of strength, while their elders discussed the crops, prices, local politics and the prospects of the ensuing year. The elderly women extended the circulation of the local gossip of the neighbourhood, while the younger ones were ready for the dance, the round of country games, and the repartee of flirtation.'

THE LONG WEEKEND

Many Canadian public holidays occur on Fridays or Mondays to give people the opportunity of enjoying a three-day weekend. This is especially important in a country where many live and work away from their families. Canadians are extremely mobile people, changing provinces, or moving from one city to another or from city centres to small towns and vice versa. The Friday preceding a long weekend is often marked by an exodus of people heading for the country (if from the city), the city (if from the country) and home, wherever that may be.

Here is a list of holidays and festivals that all Canadians celebrate:
- You can tell **Christmas and New Year** are coming when the mailman brings you a Christmas mail-order catalogue so you can

get all your gifts. This, plus the advertisements and shops, try to persuade you that Christmas begins in early November, almost as soon as Halloween ends. Then, even before December 25 arrives, you are plagued with Boxing Day sales.

In fact, Canada celebrates Christmas with a two-week holiday for schools that begins with the weekend before Christmas. For offices and businesses in most of the country, both Christmas Day (December 25) and Boxing Day (December 26) are public holidays, as is New Year's Day (January 1).

Apart from the commercialisation of the season, there is still a good deal of Christmas tradition alive. Thus parents and teachers may encourage little boys and girls to write to Santa Claus, who lives in the North Pole, making toys for them with his elves. Even Canada Post plays the game and will reply on Santa's behalf to all letters addressed to Santa Claus, North Pole, Canada, HOH OHO.

Families get together at this time, and a highlight is the Christmas dinner, often featuring a roast turkey, ham and a Christmas pudding.

- **Easter** is an extra-long weekend which begins with Good Friday (the Friday before Easter) and finishes with Easter Monday (the Monday following Easter). Although a traditionally Christian celebration, like Christmas, it has been commercialised and stores sell hot cross buns, Easter bunnies and chocolate Easter eggs when this time of the year comes around.
- **Victoria Day**, celebrating Queen Victoria's birthday, falls on the Monday before May 25.
- **Canada Day**, July 1, is the anniversary of Confederation or the creation of the Dominion of Canada in 1867. It was formerly called Dominion Day, and is the occasion for big and small celebrations of nationalism all over the country.
- Most communities in Canada also have a public holiday in August – usually the first weekend of the month – called the **August civic holiday.** As this has no special national significance, it is com-

185

monly left up to the various municipalities to declare that it will take place. It does, however, mark the mid-point of the summer season, and provides yet another opportunity for families to get away to the countryside for a long weekend.

- **Labour Day** is the first Monday in September. For school children, it is the last fling before a new school year begins. It marks the end of summer and the beginning of school.

- **Thanksgiving** is celebrated both in America and in Canada, but on different dates. In America, Thanksgiving falls on the fourth Thursday of November but in Canada, it is celebrated on the second Monday in October. It is a day of thanksgiving for a bountiful harvest.

- **Halloween** on October 31 is not a public holiday, but is a big event for children. They look forward to dressing up in costumes and going from house to house getting treats. Shops sell all kinds of Halloween costumes and offer free pumpkins. The pumpkins are hollowed out to make glowing jack o' lanterns at night. Younger children often go out accompanied by their parents or older siblings. Adults stock up on sweets and candies to give when the children come calling. Older children and teenagers often disdain 'trick and treating'. For them, Halloween is a time to throw firecrackers at passing cars perhaps, and eggs at anything. In the morning, buildings, pavements and parked cars can look a mess.

  Unfortunately for the children, some people apparently think it is 'fun' to give 'treats' of apples and candy with needles or poison in them. So parents are warned to check the candy and treats brought home before allowing children to eat them.

  If you want to get into the Halloween spirit, here are some make-up tips from a Hollywood special effects master: use corn syrup and red food colouring to make fake blood and apply it liberally on your face. Chalk or some dark eye make-up around the eyes will give you a ghoulish look. Colour your tongue and teeth with a lot of yellow and green food colouring.

'Trick or treat!' Halloween is a festival much loved by children who dress up in scary fancy dress. Notice the jack o' lantern in the bottom left hand corner.

- **Remembrance Day** is a time to parade the old uniforms and medals and remember the dead of the two world wars. It is held on November 11 because the armistice which officially ended World War I happened at the 11th hour of the 11th day of the 11th month – 11 a.m. on November 11, 1918. Members of the Royal Canadian Legion, together with other uniformed groups, gather at the court house, city hall or other town centre where the cenotaph is and pay their respects to the fallen. The ceremony often includes a religious service, the playing of the Last Post and Reveille, a traditional two-minute silence and the laying of wreaths. Remembrance Day, however, is no longer an official public holiday.

In addition to the above, there are holidays that may be celebrated in some provinces but not in others. Newfoundland seems to be the province with the greatest number of other holidays – Commonwealth Day is celebrated on the second Monday in March, and the following holidays are observed on the nearest Monday to the anniversary date – St Patrick's Day (March 17), St George's Day (April 23), Discovery Day (June 27), Memorial Day (July 7) and Orangemen's Day (July 10). Alberta has Alberta Family Day (third Monday in February) and Heritage Day (first Monday in August). Ontario, Manitoba, Saskatchewan and the Northwest Territories celebrate Civic Holiday (first Monday in August). In British Columbia, that same day is called BC Day. Quebec celebrates St Jean Baptiste Day (the patron saint of Quebec) on June 24, and the Yukon Discovery Day (third Monday in August).

– Chapter Eleven –

DOING BUSINESS IN CANADA

The impact of the United States pervades all business dealings and dictates many of the practices which are followed in organisations, both large and small.

Canadian manufacturing industries are acutely aware that the largest customer for all of Canada's products has always been the United States, and the impact of their large neighbour is felt nowhere more profoundly than in their pervasive control of the marketplace. For instance, in 1988 three of Canada's 10 largest companies were wholly US owned, while a number of other major companies had extensive American stock holdings. Although the Canadian government has tried to minimise the effect of this fact on Canadian industry over the years, it does have extensive ramifications both for those who run businesses and for those who seek jobs.

Businessmen have to be aware that the David and Goliath syndrome is very much at work in Canada. So much of Canadian business is American dominated, either physically by being a subsidiary of an American parent company or simply through the need to compete viably in a more and more North-American-oriented market, that managing any kind of business which may come into direct competition with a much bigger and better funded American one is always risky – especially in this era of free trade legislation. In hard economic times it is usually the Canadian companies which fold up first.

The impact of the United States on the Canadian employee has become frighteningly more apparent since the implementation of a free trade policy between the States and Canada in 1988. In times of plenty, free trade can mean more and greater job opportunities for the Canadian worker, but when times are not so good, jobs have a tendency to move south of the border and away from Canadian workers. This is particularly important for those who seek jobs for the first time as the seniority system is generally the yardstick which is applied in any cases of layoff. The shorter the time that a worker has had his job, the more the chance of losing it when hard times loom.

Goliath apart, however, there is still plenty of room both for the potential employer and employee in Canadian business – especially in areas related to the service sector which is much less susceptible to domination by the Americans. Those who choose to invest either their capital or their labour in Canada can be amply rewarded, both in material terms and in their quality of life, if they understand the peculiarities of the Canadian way of doing business.

ENTREPRENEURSHIP IN CANADA

In fact, the spirit of entrepreneurship has certainly been flourishing in Canada over recent years. In his book *The New Entrepreneurs*, author

The Canadian National Exhibition, held in Toronto, gives a good overview of what the Canadian industry is capable of. As it attracts many visitors, trade is brisk for the small entrepreneurs who set up stalls in the exhibition grounds.

Allan Gould lists 75 Canadian success stories in starting new and enterprising new businesses. Among those he lists are Cultures Restaurants, specialising in fresh produce served in a fast food environment; Journey's End Motels, a rapidly growing no-frills motel chain; Colours, a skin and fashion co-ordinating service started by an ex-cocktail waitress from Newfoundland; Japan Cameras, a chain of retail photography stores; College Pro, a painting and decorating service started by a college student; Noma, an electrical company which specialises in making Christmas lights; Tilley Endurables, specialising in rugged products that are guaranteed never to wear out; Annick Press, an adventurous publisher of children's books; and Homestead Computing services, which brings computer-ised technology to the family farm. All of these businesses were started in different areas of Canada by people with limited capital who used instead their knowledge and good sense to take an idea whose time had come and turn it into a viable and successful business.

STARTING A BUSINESS IN CANADA

As in any country, starting a business in Canada is always a risky proposition – especially in hard times. Out of any 100 businesses that start operation, more are going to fail than are going to make it through the first year. Of course, this obviously indicates that some are going to succeed as well – again probably those who have carefully studied the current trends of successful business in Canada.

Understanding Canadians and what they want is obviously the first step to a successful business. Service industries are always much in demand by Canadians, who are constantly looking for any ways in which a task can be done faster and more efficiently. Similarly, environmental issues are a preoccupation with the Canadian public with the result that products and services which do not pollute and in fact reduce the likelihood of this happening will be popular for some years to come. Leisure products and activities will also enjoy similar popularity as work practices change and Canadians have more time to spend on their own choice of activities.

Starting a business, however, is not just a matter of picking a product or service and hanging up a sign. Because of Canada's vast size, the ideal location is also important, depending on the nature of the product or service offered. Something which might have over-whelming success in Vancouver or the west might be completely inappropriate for eastern Canada, where both the people and their needs are different. Similarly, the manner in which a business can be started in Canada may depend on national, provincial and local regulations – depending on the province and the type of business – and even on local restrictions which could be in force. All of these considerations should be closely investigated prior to attempting to start any business. Contacting local business associations such as the Chamber of Commerce or Board of Trade – which promote business growth – can often be very helpful in these investigations. However, generally speaking, businesses in Canada can be owned in one of four ways – as a sole proprietorship, a partnership, a limited company or as a franchise.

All four of these methods of starting a business in Canada have their advantages and disadvantages and all are commonly used methods – the choice of which method to use usually depends on the proposed size of the business to be started and the capital available to start it with. Financial assistance to start a new business is usually available from either the federal or provincial government through such agencies as the Federal Business Development Bank, Provincial Development Corporations or through special legislation such as the Small Business Loans Act, which allows specially underwritten low cost loans to be obtained through the Canadian chartered banks.

Sole Proprietorship

The sole proprietorship is a business owned by one person only who is legally responsible for all its debts and other obligations. To start a business in this way usually requires only a permit from the local

193

municipality to operate and the willingness to observe all the necessary regulations concerning operating hours, employment practices and fire and sanitary requirements. The great advantage is the ease of operation – there is no one else to consult and the owner is completely free to make any decisions he thinks fit whenever he feels they are appropriate. Financially too, the sole proprietorship has some advantages – the sole owner need not publish a financial statement as companies are obliged to do, as the annual net income from his business is included in his own personal income tax return, which is a private document.

Partnership

A partnership can be one of two kinds – a general partnership in which all the partners share equally in the management of the business and the profits and have unlimited liability for any losses incurred; on the other hand, a limited partnership limits the liability for loss of some of the partners to the amount which they have invested in the partnership. General partners – of which there must be at least one in any partnership – can be either active (a partner whose name appears in the firm's name), dormant (someone who has an interest in the business but whose name does not appear in the firm's name) or ostensible (someone who lends his name to a partnership, but has no financial interest in it). In most provinces, the setting up of a partnership must be registered within a specified period of time, and the partners are encouraged – and in some cases required – to file at the same time a written agreement of partnership in case of any later disputes among the partners. Partners often find it easier to raise funds through the chartered banks or other loan agencies as there are at least two or more talents involved in running the business, although there are obviously some individual disadvantages when it comes to spending this money as its disbursement must be agreed upon by all the partners. As with the sole proprietorship no special tax returns have to be filed with the government.

Limited Company

The limited company, or business corporation, is a more complicated way of starting business, but in some way also a safer one. A limited company can be registered either with the federal government – if business is to be done in more than one province – or with a specific province if the operations are limited to that province alone. Incorporation is possible as either a private stock company (up to 49 stockholders) or as a public stock company, whose charter determines the maximum number of stockholders and permits trading on any of the three public stock exchanges. Limited companies can be established in one of four ways: by special act of the federal parliament (such corporations as banks, etc.), through adherence to the terms of some special act of a provincial parliament (loans and trust companies, for instance), by incorporation under the federal Canada Business Corporations Act or through a provincial Corporations Act. Federal incorporation requires the registration with the federal government of information on the location of the head office, the names of the directors and the ways in which shares in the company are to be issued and divided. Provincial incorporation is achieved either through a registration system or a letters patent system, depending on the province. But both procedures require the filing of information concerning location, directors and shareholders. The financial affairs of a limited company have to be declared and made available to all the shareholders and regular annual reports must be issued. The main advantage of a limited company is the fact that all the shareholders are limited in their liability only to the amount which they have paid for their shares, and thus, in case of financial trouble in the company, their personal assets are not at risk.

Franchise

A very popular way of entering business in Canada is through the purchase of a franchise operation. A franchise is a licence to operate a business which has already established its name and proved that it

195

has a good and expanding market. The food industry, especially fast foods, has traditionally been an area in which franchising is a common practice, and this is now extending to all facets of the service industry structure. When a franchise is purchased, it is often on a turnkey basis, which means that training and facilities are provided by the franchisor to the purchaser, who follows a strict set of guidelines laid down by the owner of the franchise in operating the business. If these guide-lines are followed and the right location has been chosen, chances are the business will have much greater success than an unknown company whose products have not yet been available on the market in other locations. To protect themselves, however, local franchise holders usually also incorporate themselves as an independent private stock company, thus limiting their liability.

FINDING A JOB

There are many different ways of finding a job in Canada, and businesses and companies will use one or a combination of these to find employees, depending on who they are looking for and where the company is located.

For management level employees, the most common place to find out about possible openings is through the advertisement columns of national, provincial or local newspapers. The Toronto *Globe and Mail* carries nationally advertised positions according to clearly defined categories, either placed directly by the company or by employment agencies (sometimes called 'headhunters'), and which invite applicants to apply in writing for a specific position, which may often involve a substantial relocation. Candidates for these positions will usually have to be well qualified in their field and have a university degree or similar academic qualifications. A personal résumé or CV (curriculum vitae) will usually also be required to be submitted with any application, prior to the short-listed candidates being called for an interview. In fact, having an impressive personal résumé available can be extremely important, especially in hard economic times, as many advertised jobs attract literally hundreds of applicants, and many employers will short-list candidates for interview on the impression created by these résumés. There are even professional résumé preparation companies which, for a fee, will make sure your personal presentation is eye-catching!

For those wishing to restrict their job search to a specific region of the country or to a more local area, provincial and local newspapers provide similar information on job opportunities, as does the local office of the Canada Employment Centre. Jobs at all levels are placed with these federally-run employment centres and the screening of applicants is usually done by them. These centres are also heavily involved in retraining and upgrading programmes for workers who find it hard to get jobs in their fields. Finally perhaps, there is no substitute for old-fashioned leg work in the job search, as a high percentage of vacant jobs never get advertised at all and it is the diligent seeker who often unearths such vacancies and benefits from the employment that they can provide.

The actual application process for a job varies, again according to the location, the company and the type of position. It could require some or all of the following: filling out a specific application form, having a preliminary interview, completing various aptitude tests required by the company, having an investigation conducted by the organisation into previous employment, a medical examination and/ or a follow-up interview by a panel of people. Certain questions and practices are not allowed by law during the hiring process in Canada – for instance, no applicant has to state his religious or sexual preference nor is any discrimination allowed in hiring on the basis of sex, race, creed or age.

Working for a Living
Those who succeed in obtaining a job find that they are usually paid either weekly or fortnightly. However, regardless of whether you are paid an hourly rate, a salary or on a commission basis, certain

deductions will inevitably be made from the pay cheque of all employees by the employer for various reasons: income tax, pension plans and specific forms of medical insurance, for example. All these deductions will be itemised in the pay statement, and the remaining money paid to the employee either in the form of a cheque or directly by pre-organised deposits into a specific account which has been opened by the employee with some kind of financial institution, such as a bank or credit union.

Some employees may be required to join some form of staff association as part of their employment, but this is usually conditional on an agreement that the employer has with his staff, and the terms of such memberships will be made clear to the new employee as soon as he begins work. The purpose of any union or federation (similar to such organisations in other parts of the world) is to protect the employee and make sure that he or she is not the victim of any discrimination or unfair practices. Trade unions exist in many fields in Canada, and among the largest are the teachers' federations, public employees' unions, automotive workers' unions and steel workers' unions. All of these organisations undertake collective bargaining on behalf of their members or oversee such bargaining and represent individual members in the event of disputes with management.

There are also a number of laws which regulate the manner in which a business can operate in Canada and what can be reasonably expected of an employee. The Canada Labour Code requires that there be no discrimination in either hiring or employment; that female workers must be paid the same as a man for the same work; that specific maximum hours of work and minimum rates of pay must be observed depending on the province; that safe working conditions must be provided for all employees; and that bargaining for wages and working conditions must be conducted in good faith and be subject to an arbitration process if negotiations become deadlocked.

For the worker who might be injured on the job, a Workmen's Compensation system is also operative. This body provides a guaranteed income for any worker who has to take time away from work due to a work related injury, and also arranges for retraining for any worker who is permanently unable to return to his former occupation. Similarly, benefit packages provided by employers to their employees often tend to be generous, including such items as long term disability insurance, life insurance and dental or optical services.

Job Security

All employees, whether seasonal or not, who are hired by their employers on an hourly or weekly basis are vulnerable to downturns in the economy which may make their jobs less secure. In the event of a company making some of its workers redundant, seniority is usually the determining criteria for layoff, with those most recently hired being the first to go. Unions will try and prevent as many workers being laid off as possible, and will support those of their members who are, but layoffs do still occur in hard times. Government programmes such as unemployment insurance exist to cushion the impact of being laid off and in many cases those laid off will be called back to work as soon as the economic climate improves.

If a worker is laid off or dismissed after having worked for a business for a specified period of time, he may also be entitled to severance pay (this depends on the circumstances of the termination and the level of the job) and is certainly entitled to unemployment insurance benefits – for which payments will have been deducted during the period of employment – which continue either until he has found another job or until a specific period of time has elapsed, after which local welfare systems can help the worker who has fallen on exceptionally hard times and is unable to find another job.

For those whose employment is permanently terminated, most employers will provide assistance with finding a new job, and will often sponsor some form of retraining programme – many of which are available through government sources in any case – to help him find another job successfully even in a new field of work.

Farming work can be found in the rural communities of the prairie provinces. Here herring gulls are searching for worms in a newly cultivated field.

TYPES OF WORK IN CANADA

Canada's economy has traditionally been resource based, and certain occupations have long been practised. Farming, fishing, mining and logging still account for a large number of jobs in Canada, but there are a number of other areas in which there are now a large number of Canadian jobs to be had, especially in the service industries.

Jobs in resource industries are found mainly in the farming, fishing, mining and logging areas of the country. Farming employment can be found in most provinces although it tends to be centred around the prairie provinces of Manitoba, Alberta and Saskatchewan, while fishing is centred on the east and west coasts, mining in the maritime provinces, and logging in the interior of British Columbia. Employment can also be found in the oil and gas industries of Alberta although jobs are not as plentiful now as they once were, and many

Canadian oil experts have gone overseas to work for much higher salaries.

The manufacturing base of the country is located in the southern section of the province of Ontario, stretching from Windsor in the southwest to the Quebec boundary on the eastern side of the province. Heavy manufacturing is located in the Toronto-Hamilton area where the majority of the automobile factories and their suppliers, including the steel industry, are situated. Most of the more recent high-tech industry is also located in the Toronto area, while the smaller centres which are connected to Toronto by the MacDonald Cartier Freeway, the main road artery of the region, have a number of light industrial plants providing an infrastructure of jobs for their communities. Manufacturing jobs can also be found in other major Canadian centres especially around Montreal and Vancouver, but outside these areas, they are scarcer and usually less well paid.

The service industry sector is the fastest growing in the country, and Canada is well on the way to having a mainly service-based economy. Tourism (including the hotel and restaurant industry) and management consultancy are two of the biggest service areas in the country and employment can be found all over the country in these industries, especially for those who have prior experience. Most of the new businesses which are starting in Canada are also service based – many of them addressing environmental concerns.

Jobs for which there are predetermined Canadian standards – not always the same as the standards which prevail overseas – are more difficult to enter for newcomers to the country. The Canadian Medical Association has strict standards for doctors who wish to practise in this country as do the associations of other health professionals. Teachers and lawyers also require special certification by the province, which has to be obtained before seeking employment and which may require some degree of retraining or a competitive examination before it can be achieved.

COMMON MANAGEMENT STRATEGIES

Management and direction in Canadian business has become very much more decentralised in recent years than it used to be. The strict hierarchy in which the boss makes the decisions and then passes his wishes down the chain of command for implementation has almost passed, and much encouragement is now given for appropriate decisions to be made by the employee, in consultation with his peers if necessary. Strategies such as those of 'quality circles' are commonly employed and divergent thinking encouraged as long as it complements the ultimate aims of the company.

This means that most Canadian managers, whether of large or small industries, have a vested interest in keeping their employees both efficient and contented. Many companies encourage substantial employee input into decision making and provide opportunities for their workers to upgrade or refine their skills at regular intervals so that they have the knowledge and the tools to be productive and useful. Safety concerns are also strictly regulated and attended to, with any job which requires any kind of exposure to hazards being strictly monitored.

Companies also sometimes assume responsibility for any problems in the behaviour of any employee. Problems with absenteeism, alcohol or drugs, or problems with fellow workers, which might in the past have resulted in dismissal, are now often dealt with through special employee assistance plans, which give the employee a chance to come to grips with and change any disruptive behaviour before facing any long-term disciplinary action. Even problems within a worker's family which could be affecting his performance on the job are sometimes dealt with by this method as companies realise that their best resource is a productive and contented worker, as free from stress as the demands of the job will allow.

CANADIAN BUSINESS ETIQUETTE

Whether you are a manager or a worker, the way in which you will be expected to conduct yourself in the workplace is not far different from business practices prevailing in most westernised societies.

For instance, the way in which you dress should be appropriate to the job that you are doing. Managers and executives are expected to come to work conservatively dressed – a suit or jacket and tie for men, an appropriate dress or pant suit for women – while those who are required to wear some form of uniform to denote their position will usually be supplied with one by their employer. Production workers may or may not be provided with working clothes, and if not, are usually free to wear more or less what they like, provided no part of their attire (including their hair) presents any kind of safety hazard.

Working hours in Canada again conform to the acceptable western standards, usually 8.30/9.00 a.m. in the morning to 4.30/5.00 p.m. in the evening, five days a week. Those in service industries, espe-

The construction industry is one in which part-time jobs are usually available, if you do not mind working out of doors.

203

cially the retail and banking business, may be required to work on Saturdays from time to time, but often, part-time workers are used to replace or supplement workers in businesses which open late or on weekends. In fact, there is a great deal of part-time work available in most Canadian centres, although much of it is low-paying and often taken by students who wish to work in their non-school hours.

The working day usually includes scheduled meal and rest breaks, 15 – 20 minutes morning and afternoon and one hour for lunch. Most working locations provide some form of rest area for their staff, and larger companies often have a caféteria which serves reasonably priced food at appropriate times. One word of caution, however – many of these areas are now designated as non-smoking locations, and some companies, in fact, have outlawed smoking on the premises completely. There is still a certain amount of controversy about this in the workplace, but, at the very least, smokers had better be prepared to find restrictions on when and where they can smoke!

Managers and executives may often be required to host and/or attend business lunches and dinners for visiting delegations or clients, which are usually held away from the office. These are usually low-key get-togethers at a local restaurant, at which routine items of business are dealt with or sales are concluded, but the formal business dinner does exist and managers will be expected to attend them whenever or wherever they may be held. Travel is often a part of an executive's job description as well, and, because of the size of the country and its close business relationship with the United States, travel on business can often involve going a considerable distance and therefore frequent overnight stays.

Most companies are also most concerned about staff development and require their employees to attend upgrading courses and work-shops on a regular basis. This too can involve travel to attend conferences and meetings in locations away from the home office. However, as the time used for this purpose is generally considered to be part of the overall working requirement, fees and expenses for staff development purposes are often absorbed by the company, with no charge or deductions to the employee.

Meetings and consultations, for whatever purposes, are very much part of the working environment in Canada and nearly all employees, no matter what position, will find occasions when they become involved. Most businesses encourage their employees to participate as much as they can in ensuring that the work of the company goes smoothly, and often have in-house committees which meet regularly for that purpose. Most Canadian meetings are not unduly lengthy and there are no special rules for their conduct other than to be prepared and to follow the directions of the chairman on whose shoulders the smooth running of any meeting rests. Participants are encouraged to speak their minds and to say what they feel – within the obvious limits of politeness and decorum – and to achieve a consensus acceptable to everybody on the points being discussed. At most meetings, there is no expectation for newcomers to be particularly reticent, but, of course, it is important that you familiarise yourself with all aspects of the issue at hand before voicing an opinion! Those who don't or who try to monopolise meetings will usually be put in their place by the chairman, who will endeavour to ensure that all points of view are heard and that the whole meeting is conducted in a fair and constructive manner.

Equality in the workplace is considered to be an important right and is respected by most Canadian employers and workers. No one should be made to feel in any way 'inferior' or 'subservient' to anyone else, including the boss, and obvious discrimination or harassment of any kind – racial, sexual or religious – is usually severely dealt with, especially if, as is often the case, it contravenes laws and/or practices specifically put in place to prevent that happening.

Chapter Twelve

THE CANADIAN MOSAIC

Like many people in developed countries, Canadians as a whole have the luxury of being able to go beyond the bread and butter problems of everyday living and to devote much of their attention to matters such as the cleaning and greening of the environment, freedom of speech, and minority rights – all issues that are often hotly debated and defended whenever they arise.

AN ENVIRONMENT CONSCIOUS SOCIETY

It may seem fitting that a country like Canada, with such a huge pulp and paper industry, should have a voracious appetite for the products it manufactures – government agencies and organisations, industries and business companies of every kind produce masses of booklets, pamphlets and advertisements to inform, explain and exhort the public to see their various points of view.

Visit the office of a government agent and you will find pamphlets containing all manner of information for every person conceivable – information for employers from the Workers' Compensation Board, a call to youth to join the Environment Youth Corps, budget explanations for the taxpayer from the Ministry of Finance, quick facts about the province from the Public Affairs Bureau, road maps, camping maps and forestry maps, a guide for parents through the changing educational system, information on programmes and benefits for seniors, regulations regarding rental housing, a how-to guide for someone contemplating a bed and breakfast business and, just in case, advice on how to Help Yourself Survive A Tsunami!

When you look into your letter box and open the morning's newspaper, you are often inundated by junk mail and flyers, which advertise every conceivable product – you are informed about the latest bargains at the supermarket and department store, appealed to for help from the many charities, cajoled to try some miracle hair growth product, enticed to get your gas from competing service stations by money-saving coupons. Even the local Member of Parliament adds to the paper pile with an 'I have your interests at heart' letter accompanied by a complimentary calendar at the end of the year while the funeral parlour tries to have the last word on how to avoid 'disadvantages when arrangements are made at time of need'!

Most of this eventually ends up in the bin. One newspaper reader wrote to say that he decided to find out how much junk mail he received. After keeping his flyers, newspaper inserts and junk mail for one month, he found the stack measured 21 centimetres!

Paper – newspapers, packaging, telephone books, glossy magazines, mail-order catalogues, etc. – makes up about 40% by weight, and about 50% by volume, of garbage. Plastics are estimated to be 8%

by weight and 30% by volume of garbage. The reason for the small percentage by weight of plastics is not because there is less plastic being used but because technology has produced lighter and more crushable plastics that are used in packaging today. The Canadian lifestyle is one that includes all kinds of plastic packaged products – fast foods in take-away throw-away boxes, bubble packs of cosmetics, soft drink or soda pop bottles, polystyrene trays of meat and vegetables, etc. Much of what is manufactured from Canada's ample resources ends in massive landfill sites where this waste material – some of it harmful or toxic – is simply buried beneath the earth and allowed to decompose. Yard waste makes up 18%, metals 10%, food waste 8% and rubber and leather 2% by weight of the solid wastes that find their way to the landfill. However, decomposition is a slow process and some materials either decompose so slowly or do not decompose at all that they create a serious environmental threat to the country's ecology.

There is no doubt, however, that Canadians are becoming more environment conscious. The media do their part in this effort. Open the newspaper or switch on the television, and you often find a feature on cleaning up the environment, tips on how to be environment friendly, the preservation of forests, the effects of acid rain, the greenhouse effect, the disappearing ozone layer and more. Manufacturers must also jump on the bandwagon to retain the goodwill of the swelling ranks of the environmentalists. More household products, especially, are being sold in packaging which manufacturers claim are recyclable or biodegradable. Thus when out shopping, you might receive your purchases in a plastic bag that proudly advertises that it is 100% biodegradable. However, '100% biodegradable' does not mean that the plastic will ever be broken down completely, but that it will be broken into pieces small enough for them not to be noticeable. Eggs come in cartons that say 'made with no CFCs'. CFCs are chlorofluorocarbons that are responsible for the depletion of the ozone layer in our atmosphere.

Canadians are becoming more and more environment conscious and they are doing their best to preserve what was given to them by Nature.

Reduce, re-use and recycle – these are three words which have become much used by Canadians over the last decade in an effort to remedy the situation, and in recognition of the fact that it has become both an environmental and economic necessity to impose more stringent standards on the disposal of materials and to encourage the re-use and recycling of products where this was practical.

Practically speaking, this means that an environment-conscious family living in Canada must be prepared to take the time and trouble to live up to its conviction that a cleaner world is the responsibility of every individual. The first step is taken when you, as a consumer, go shopping. As practically everything you buy comes in packaging that will end up in the bin, environmentalists suggest that you buy carefully, for example, choosing something that comes in a recyclable container rather than an equivalent product in a plastic blister pack. In addition to what you bring home, there is, as mentioned earlier, a tremendous flood of unsolicited material that arrives on your doorstep or is put into your mailbox. Everything needs to be disposed of, but hopefully not in a landfill site. In most Canadian towns and cities, household garbage is picked up only once a week. The householder must therefore find the space and take the time to sort and store all recyclable items in his home till he is able to dispose of them in an environmentally safe way.

The Blue Box

Many Canadian communities have adopted the blue box programme, in which each municipality is responsible for establishing a plant in which various kinds of waste products – particularly paper, glass and tin – can be processed for re-use in other forms. Each household is issued with a blue box into which items that can be recycled are placed for collection. The blue boxes are emptied at the same time when regular household garbage is picked up, but instead of ending up in massive landfill sites, those items that can be re-used are treated appropriately.

Even in communities where there is no blue box programme, recycling is fast becoming a part of the lifestyle. Environmental organisations do what they can to encourage people to collect recyclable items and bring them to a collection depot. The types of recyclables accepted depend on the services available in the community, but generally, you are asked to rinse out containers, remove contaminants, and sort the different types of recyclable items first. Paper products are separated into different types such as newspapers, flyers, office paper, high quality paper like computer paper, and cardboard. Sometimes some items like plasticised and waxed paper, styrofoam and certain types of glass may not be acceptable. The demands of each recycling depot vary, and it takes some patience and commitment to the cause to become a dedicated recycler.

The kitchen is one place in the home which generates lots of garbage. Some households have a 'garburettor' installed to deal with this problem. The 'garburettor' is fitted to the bottom of the kitchen sink, where, at the flick of a switch, it will grind up most kitchen waste, even chicken bones, so that it can be flushed into the sewer system. It is even better to collect such kitchen wastes as fruit and vegetable peelings, egg shells and other organic material (but not fats or cooked foods) for composting in the garden together with grass clippings, leaves, wood shavings and ash from the fireplace.

Supermarkets have bins to take back all the plastic shopping bags that their customers have used, for recycling. In many cities, there are leaf collection and composting programmes in the fall, during which householders are encouraged to collect their leaves in bags for picking up and recycling. Soft drink and beer bottles and cans can be returned to their place of purchase or to a bottle depot for a refund, 'white goods' or old refrigerators, stoves, washers and dryers are sent to a depot or second-hand dealer, used motor oil collected and sent to a service station which accepts it, and clean clothing in a usable condition can be donated to charitable organisations and second-hand stores.

THE SEXUAL ISSUE

During the last decade, sexual equality has become a most important issue in Canada. Women, who were comparatively recently thought of as 'second class citizens', have begun to occupy a more just place in Canadian society, in both a moral and a practical sense. Nowhere more so has this been true than in the workplace, which has seen ever increasing numbers of women begin to move towards and occupy some of the most powerful and prestigious positions in public life.

Women at Work

Like many other countries, Canada's attitude towards women in the workplace was for many years patronising, to say the least. It was felt that there were certain jobs that were by some kind of unexplained right properly male – usually those that either demanded physical strength or which involved management skills – and there were similarly other jobs to which women were more properly suited (nursing, teaching etc.). For decades, this way of thinking was never really challenged.

By the 1990s, however, there has been a significant and most timely change both in male attitudes and in the number of women occupying key positions in all sectors of the economy. More women are leaving their homes to work. In 1945, only one in four Canadian women worked outside their homes. Today, half of all Canadian women are employed in the workforce and it is estimated that, if the present trend continues, about two-thirds of all women over the age of 20 will be working by the year 2000. Much of this change has been brought about by a change in society's vision of the role of women and by women's perceptions of themselves, aided by significant legislation which has made this change both possible and permanent. Canada now has a Charter of Rights which forbids sexual discrimination in hiring and promotion, and pay equity legislation mandating equal pay for equal work regardless of gender is now on the books in most Canadian provinces. However, in spite of such legislation, some

Canadian Mounties in training. Note the person in the middle. Yes! Women are a part of the Royal Canadian Mounted Police as well.

women in the workforce still earn less than their male counterparts.

There is also, unfortunately, still a dearth of women in some traditionally male professions – engineering and medicine, for instance – although there has been a significant growth in others, such as education and law. Serious efforts are being directed at attracting women into those jobs into which they have not traditionally gone, and similarly to encourage men to take on roles which they have hitherto shunned. However, the process is slow and it will take at least a generation before the impact of this process is really felt. To encourage women to enter and remain in the workforce in greater numbers, such provisions as maternity benefits and pensions have been overhauled, and there is now even provision in many places of employment for paternity leave to enable the man to shoulder his share of child rearing. A husband and wife sharing one job, providing they hold equivalent qualifications, is not unknown, nor is the concept

213

of the househusband where the man stays at home while the woman goes out to work.

Sexual Harassment

The issue of sexual harassment in the work place has also been addressed. In the past, women workers were often forced to endure sexual innuendo and sometimes even physical abuse by their male colleagues, but strict legislation has brought this situation under control in most places, so that this kind of practice has been substantially reduced.

The Changing Role of Women

Outside the workplace, the role of women is also changing, particularly as so many of them are now employed on a full time basis, either through choice or economic necessity. The Canadian male now expects to shoulder his share of the domestic chores – although statistically it is still the woman who does the lion's share – and to be actively involved in the child rearing process. Domestic violence is still an issue in some homes, however, but once again there is now a greater awareness of the problem in society at large, and more provisions both legal and societal to deal with it. In most homes, both boys and girls are brought up to believe that – apart from physical differences – there are few differences in capability between men and women and that most tasks in life can be performed equally by people of either sex. It will take another generation or two for this attitude to permeate Canadian society thoroughly but the process is well started. The achievement of as total a sexual equality as possible is a goal that is actively sought by the majority of Canadians and is supported by the policies of the governments which represent them.

Famous Canadian Women

Canadian feminists have many models to emulate in their fight for justice and equality, not least of which were the 'Famous Five' –

Emily Murphy, Henrietta Muir Edwards, Louise McKinney, Irene Parlby and Nellie McClung – who challenged the law of the land.

Emily Murphy, born in 1868, was the wife of an Anglican pastor in Manitoba. She was one of the first advocates of feminism in Canada, campaigning for the property rights of married women, as well as for a women's court in which women involved in legal cases could testify without suffering embarrassment. When the first such court was established in the province of Alberta in 1916, Emily Murphy became the first woman magistrate in the British Empire and presided over it. Later that year, another woman, Alice Jamieson, was made magistrate in Calgary, but both positions were challenged by Alberta lawyers who argued that women were not legally 'persons' and could therefore not hold public office. Although the appointments were upheld by the Supreme Court of Alberta, this was not necessarily so in the rest of Canada. Emily Murphy and four other women therefore decided to challenge this and formally asked the Supreme Court of Canada for judgment on whether a woman could have a seat in Senate. The other four women were Henrietta Muir Edwards, a founding member of the National Council of Women, Louise McKinney, a former Alberta Member of Legislative Assembly, Irene Parlby, an Alberta cabinet minister, and Nellie McClung, another Alberta MLA. Together, they became known as the 'Famous Five'. When the Supreme Court decided that women could not be senators, the five appealed to the Privy Council in England, which ruled in 1929 that women were 'persons'. The following year, Cairine Wilson became the first woman to be appointed senator.

FREEDOM OF SPEECH

Freedom of speech is another issue close to the heart of Canadians. Like their American neighbours, Canadians strongly believe in their right to speak out freely and without fear on issues which interest, annoy or frustrate them. Criticism of government policies and practices is commonly voiced both in public and private, and those who voice them do so without fear of retribution.

There are, of course, laws in Canada against both attacking someone with unjustified personal accusations either in print (libel) or by making unfounded and damaging verbal accusations (slander). Those who do this can be arrested and prosecuted. Politicians speaking in the House of Commons are exempted from this law, but otherwise it applies everywhere in the country and to everybody.

The press in Canada jealously guards its right to be free to say what it thinks and so newspapers, radio and television regularly discuss any topics which are timely and relevant. Their opinions do not always reflect or agree with those voiced by the government – nor even by the majority of Canadians – but the ideas and opinions voiced in the media are considered as an important part of determining the national position on matters both domestic and international. Naturally, there are some restrictions on offending public taste in public media to protect those who find some material offensive, though the issue of censorship is never very far below the surface in this regard and is one over which not everyone is in agreement!

Freedom of speech is seen by most Canadians as an important part of their democratic way of life, and both long-term residents and newcomers value their right to voice their opinion whenever it's appropriate to do so without fear of retribution – though always being prepared for an argument with those who do not agree with them!

LIVING IN THE CANADIAN MOSAIC

Having discussed many of the things that make up Canada, such as the physical characteristics of the land, its history, the composition of Canadians, native as well as immigrant, and what they like to do, eat and how they socialise, there are still many other elements that characterise the Canadian lifestyle, pieces that when added to the picture help complete the colourful mosaic of Canada and its people, such as ...

A Question of Size

Huge, huge, HUGE – remember the word 'humongous'? It describes the country and many things about it. Some humongous things are …

- **Buying in bulk**. In a large supermarket, you can usually find a section that sells almost anything in huge containers – soft drinks (or 'pop' as it is called here), pickles, condiments, flour, bird seed, etc. The customer takes just as much or as little as is needed. The advantage of this is you can buy any amount you like, without being limited by the manufacturer's packaging. Many other items, such as meat, are sold in family size quantities at prices that allow you to take advantage of the economy of size.

- **'Big wheels'**. Especially in the small towns and in the country, a common mode of transport is a truck or a 4x4 (four-wheel drive) vehicle. These are usually vehicles used for work, or on the farms. But it's surprising to see a huge monster of a truck go by with a little old lady at the wheel.

- **'Big money'**. This is what you have to pay for almost any kind of service. When you need some electrical or plumbing work done in your home, for example, you learn what expensive labour is all about. This is culture shock that hits the wallet. We had the electrician come and put in some wiring and heaters, a job which took less than a day's work, under five hours. When the bill came, it was a whopping C$300 plus.

The Honour System

Much in Canada works on the honour system, that is, a system that does not depend so much upon authority, policing or penalties, as upon trust. It is a system that has evolved from the fact that many areas are vastly under-populated and often there isn't the manpower to keep a lot of activities and services functioning. So the honour system has had to be relied upon. People are expected to 'do the right thing' even when there is nobody looking.

Many of the examples of how the honour system works will

In many isolated areas of Canada, the honour system is part of the way of life.

obviously be found in the country rather than urban areas, such as at private as well as public campsites in the wilderness where campers are expected to deposit the camping fee into a money box because park rangers are not always on site. Numerous recreational facilities are provided for the enjoyment of many by a dedicated few who volunteer their time for the love of it, such as a ski group that maintains the trails outside a nearby town in the winter. These people are not able to collect fees from those who enjoy the fruits of their labour, but trust in the goodwill of skiers to give what they can towards the maintenance of such facilities into an 'honour box' at the start of the trail.

A woman whose interest in apiculture (the raising of honey bees) has evolved from a hobby into a small business, sells honey from her home. As this is a part-time business, and she and her husband have other work, this is done simply by putting jars of honey in a wooden shed by the gate, together with a money box and a sign displaying the prices. Customers are expected to serve themselves and put the correct amount of money into the box. This honour system has worked very well, she says, as most people are honest.

While there are always people who try to take advantage and beat the system, Canadians generally having grown up with the honour system accept that if there is any cheating, it is to no one's benefit. Thus even at the customs checkpoint at the US border, the honour system is used (though this is supplemented by the eagle eye of an experienced customs officer). Border crossings are facilitated with a minimum of red tape. When returning from the south, you are asked how many days you have been out of the country and there is nothing in your passport to verify whatever information you might give. Canadian citizens don't even need passports to go across to the United States. And in the latest move, the federal government is trying a new system that will hopefully reduce traffic jams at the border – for a fee of C$10, you can use an express lane to return to Canada, skipping the customs checkpoint. Instead you are honour bound to declare your dutiable items on a form, drop it into a box, and have the amount you owe debited from your credit card.

Rights of the Consumer

Canadians are very conscious of their rights. Canadian laws ensure that the consumer's interests are protected by fair advertising and packaging and that market standards are kept. There are federal as well as provincial departments that one could go to with a complaint if one's consumer rights have been violated. In addition, there is a Consumers' Association of Canada that helps people who have problems resulting from buying goods and services. However, these are avenues of last resort and, hopefully, should not be necessary. In fact, many stores (especially those that are part of a big chain) and their sales personnel seldom object when you have bought something from the store and wish to return it, if you have a good reason for doing so. Thus, a shirt or dress could be returned not only if there was an obvious flaw in it but even if you later decided you did not like the colour after all. Those who come from countries where the rights of a customer are vigorously defended may think nothing of this, but there are others who find such consideration enough of a novelty to be worthy of mention. Naturally, one's idea of a reasonable basis for wishing to return a purchase might not agree with another's, but the Canadian consumer has a fair amount of liberty, and the patience of the store management and their wish to keep their customers happy are earnest. For example, a driver who bought a new set of rims for his car brought them back, somewhat rusted, to the tyre dealer after one winter. The dealer accepted the man's argument that the rims should have lasted at least one season without showing signs of rust and offered him another set in exchange. Stores seldom argue with the customer, but it is best if you have a receipt that proves you bought the item from that particular store, and they will almost always exchange the faulty item or give you a refund. Some stores, however, have a 'no cash refunds, exchanges only' policy and others do stipulate a time limit within which any goods that you are not satisfied with should be returned. It is important to make a note of such policies when buying from these stores.

The Luck of the Draw

'B 6, I 23, N 35, G 50, O 71 ...' the voice calls. In the hall, long tables take up almost every space, with just enough room for chairs back to back. Thick smoke fills the air. As many as 100 to 200 people gather for bingo, at a different place each night of the week. It could be the Canadian Legion hall, church hall, civic centre or seniors' residential home. The games are complex and not really for the uninitiated because you have to be fast with the eye and quick with the hand.

Bingo is a popular form of entertainment and the games are often a means for many organisations to raise funds for their activities. If you pass by a community hall in the evening, for instance, and find a long line of cars parked outside, chances are there's probably a bingo game going on inside.

Garage Sales

You really learn what spring cleaning is when you live in a country with four seasons. After a long and cold winter during which one can feel very cooped up indoors, the gradual warming up of spring provides an opportunity to open up windows and let the fresh air in. The sunshine and warmer weather often encourage one to get some serious cleaning done. Attics, basements and garages are emptied and unwanted junk and white elephants put up for sale during weekends. Telephone poles in the centre of town sprout cardboard signs advertising garage sales. Notice boards in the local stores publicise the same. The avid bargain hunter scours these places and the classifieds in the town newspaper each Friday, so that he can be out early on Saturday morning to grab the best bargains. You learn to spot the house with the sale by the number of cars and trucks parked outside. While good purchases can certainly be made if you are a careful buyer who scrutinises each potential buy and does not succumb to every 'bargain', it is easy to come away with a handful of cheap items, only to find later that you have no use for all that junk you paid for. And if you have been weak and given in to the bargains all spring, then it's your turn to hold a garage sale of your own, so long as the weather stays sunny and warm.

Door-to-Door

Be prepared to be bothered by a lot of door-to-door canvassing, which, however, is not a phenomenon exclusive to life in Canada but is certainly a part of it. Canvassers often have good reasons or worthy causes that bring them to your door – they may be volunteers trying to raise funds for charities or community projects, children trying to sell calendars, chocolates etc. to raise money for a school outing – but there is another category of door-knockers who can get on one's nerves. These are salespeople who can become nuisances when they refuse to take 'no' for an answer. An example of such a person is the salesman who periodically canvasses around the neighbourhood, trying to convince people that a freezer full of expensive frozen convenience-gourmet food is an essential household item to have in their basement. A variation of the door-to-door salesperson is the 'telemarketer' who resorts to telephoning people and bombarding them with all sorts of advertising gimmicks.

Addressing a Postal Problem

Have you corresponded with anyone in Canada? Some people, mainly those who live in more urban areas, have 'regular' addresses, such as A. Jones, who can be reached at 123, Main Street, Townsville. But as there is a large proportion of Canadians who live in small country towns, Canada Post has had to devise a different postal system to cope with the great distances the postal worker would have to cover to get from one address to the next, and the lack of people with which to do it. The post office in town therefore usually has a separate section consisting entirely of postal boxes. Each post box would be assigned to a household in town. If your friend, therefore, has a PO Box number for his mailing address, it is not because he wishes to keep his true address a secret from you. Even stranger is the address that looks something like a code, for example, RR#1 S23 C45! Addresses consisting of such an incomprehensible cluster of letters and numbers usually belong to those who live out in the country, and can be decoded like this: RR is short for 'rural route' (of which there are many in Canada and therefore they have to be numbered); S is a specific 'site' (in this case, site number 23 along rural road 1) at which there is a 'cabinet' or cluster of post boxes and it is usually at a road junction closest to the houses it serves; C stands for the 'compartment' or box, each of which is numbered and assigned, one to each household. With such a system, the person who delivers the mail saves an enormous amount of time and energy and can deliver letters to 30 or 40 houses at a single stop.

A Manner of Greeting

'How are you today?' A girl from Hong Kong remarked that Canadians greet you by asking how you are doing. It upset her to discover that they weren't really interested in her answer. 'They expect you to say "good", "all right" or something like that and then to move on. If they don't really care how I'm doing, why ask?' she wanted to know.

Well, such disappointment can be avoided if one realises that the greeting has to be taken in the spirit of just a polite enquiry. You usually answer 'good' to this standard Canadian query, regardless of how you might really feel. That's not to say that the query is always a matter of just being polite and nothing else. Often, it might be genuine. A 'How are you today?' can often be a genuine question and a means to get to know people.

BECOMING PART OF THE MOSAIC

The United States is often described as a 'melting pot' of many cultures, while Canada is often described as a 'mosaic'. It is an image that was given wide currency by John Porter, who called his sociological study of social class and power in Canada *The Vertical Mosaic*.

For those of us who come from the big cosmopolitan cities of other countries and speak English (or French, if you are settling into the French-speaking areas of Quebec), becoming a part of the mosaic and fitting into Canadian lifestyle comes more easily. A migrant who moved from Asia to Canada said that during those first few months she had braced herself for the expected cultural impact her move would cause. But 'the most interesting thing is that I have experienced no "culture shock", but I seem to have blended right in,' she said. She attributed this to the fact that she had travelled a fair bit and lived in a big, cosmopolitan city and had consequently been exposed to much cultural diversity. 'The Canadians I have come to know (although not too many) seem to be able to talk on the same wavelength. Any difference in values and behaviour and expectations are very subtle and I haven't been able to put my finger on them yet.'

But sometimes, our cultural traits do betray us. As a Chinese radio personality once said, he would have been saved a lot of pain if someone had told him that Canadians don't like people to talk loudly (a distinctly Chinese trait, he thought). This remark brings to mind an incident that happened in a supermarket – when a particularly loud conversation between two women could be clearly heard over the normal hum of noise in the supermarket. It came from several aisles away, and the speakers could not be seen, but most certainly were heard by all in the vicinity, speaking loudly in a foreign dialect. They were most definitely the focus of curious stares from shoppers all around!

It is comforting to seek the company of people who come from the same cultural and traditional background, hence there are often clusters of ethnic groups to be found in many cosmopolitan cities, not only in Canada but in cities all over the world. But ultimately interaction with the wider world, and learning to adjust to living in a new country, even though it may take a generation or two to do it, cannot be avoided. In Canada, therefore, there are often private social and government agencies, such as Employment and Immigration Canada, that will help people newly arrived in the country to adjust to their new surroundings, counsel them and help them especially to undergo job training and find employment. Those who do not speak English, which is the language of interaction in most of Canada, are encouraged to learn it. Some schools and colleges conduct part-time and evening classes in English as a second language.

Naturally, not all newcomers to Canada will have problems adjusting to their new surroundings for various reasons – they may merely have exchanged one western tradition for a similar one in Canada, or even if they had come from an Asian country, they may not have been so steeped in their cultural traditions as to make assimilation a problem. Even so, they may want to blend into their new Canadian surroundings as quickly as possible. Besides establishing relationships at one's place of work, it is a good idea to form other circles of friends. One way to do this would be to seek out people with similar interests. A look through the local newspaper will often provide a calendar of events, covering a wide selection of recreational, social and other community organisations. It only remains for the newcomer to the area to introduce himself and participate in his chosen activities, be it that of the town's darts club, tennis club, baby clinics, motorcycle association, arts and crafts group, weight watchers or overeaters anonymous, and he will soon find himself becoming a part of his community.

CROSS-CANADA QUIZ

Are you ready for the experience that Canada will offer either the short-term visitor or long-staying friend? Here are some questions and situations for you to test yourself with:

Quiz 1

You go to the bank to open an account. The teller asks for your personal details – name, age, address, etc. – and then, she wants to know what your SIN is! You:

A Tell her you've already confessed to your priest and been absolved.

B Say it's none of her business and walk out of the bank in a huff.

C Lean across the counter to her and get it all off your chest.

Answer

None of the above! SIN is short for a Social Insurance Number which you have to apply for when you live in Canada because you need it for almost anything official, like applying for a job, joining a medical plan or pension fund, or opening a bank account. It is an identification number and looks something like this: 737 911 595. That's what the bank teller wants from you!

Quiz 2

You have accepted an invitation to a pot-luck supper for members of the ABC club and their families. On the night of the supper, you:

A Bring a big empty pot so that with luck you can go back home with it loaded full of goodies.

B Ask the organiser how many people are expected to attend and bring a big pot of stew that will be enough to feed the whole company and more.

C Bring a dish that you have cooked, but is just enough to feed you and your family.

Answer

It might appear selfish to bring just enough for you and your family only, but *C* is the correct answer. You put your offering on the main table where all the food is spread, and then go about sampling all the interesting items that have been contributed by the other guests. Potluck suppers are based on the theory that if everyone brings enough food for himself, there will be sufficient to feed the company, and there usually is a lot left over too.

Quiz 3

You are driving in a small Canadian town and someone suddenly crosses the road in front of you without even looking at you. You:
A Stop and allow him to cross.

B Let him cross but sound your horn in justified anger, stick your head out the window and tell him to look where he's going.

C Decide you'll teach him a lesson in road safety by stepping on the accelerator and narrowly missing him as he jumps back in alarm.

Answer

The pedestrian always has the right of way, and he can cross the road at any point, not only at junctions, and expect that the motorist will let him pass. This is especially so in a small town. He also has the right of way in the city, but will have a hard time convincing the motorists of this fact. It would be best and most courteous to do *A*. You will find that many small-town Canadian drivers are extremely patient. Some might do *B* but you should never choose *C*.

Quiz 4

Still driving in that small Canadian town, you approach a junction and notice that there are two vehicles blocking the way, their drivers having an animated conversation. You:

A   Assume that one of the drivers is lost and is getting directions from the other, and toot your horn to remind them there's somebody waiting to pass.
B   Assume that this is a chance encounter between two old friends who haven't seen each other for 10 years or more, toot your horn and tell them to go to the nearest café where they can continue their conversation while you hurry on to your urgent appointment.
C   Assume neither A nor B but wait patiently behind till they are ready to move on.

Answer

You will know by now that *C* is the correct answer. Curb the urge to press the horn, because it is not polite and restrained, as Canadians like to be. Be assured that when the drivers realise there is someone waiting for them to go, they will limit their conversation (hopefully to not more than five minutes) and move on!

Quiz 5

You have now left the town and are driving along a country road when suddenly a deer jumps in front of your car. No matter how quickly you react, you cannot avoid the animal and hit it. You:

A   Recover from your fright and drive on, since it was only a deer and nobody else got hurt.

B   Recover from your fright and drive to the nearest police station to make a report.

C   Recover from your fright, toss the dead animal into the trunk of your car and bring it home for a venison supper.

Answer

It's against the law to do *C*. And no doubt, lots of people decide to do *A* even though *B* is the correct course of action and the most public-spirited thing to do, because *B* entails taking a lot of time and trouble. But it is really best to drive carefully, especially in the very rural parts of the country and at around dusk when your chances of encountering wildlife on the highways are greatest. The consequences can be serious if you should hit a large animal such as a moose!

Quiz 6

You are visiting St John's in Newfoundland and enter a department store to look for some souvenirs. A sweat-shirt catches your eye, and the price tag says C$24, just what you can afford. You stand in line at the cashier's and when it's your turn to pay, the cash register rings and the cashier tells you your bill comes to C$28.56! You are shocked and embarrassed, because you only have $26 in your wallet. You:

A   Get all huffy with the cashier, point to the price tag and demand an explanation.

B   Retreat in confusion as quickly as you can, without finding out why there was such a discrepancy in the sale price.

C   Realise that once again, you have forgotten that there are hidden costs to add to the price of the sweat-shirt.

Answer

If you don't know why you had to pay an extra C$4.56, you should ask for an explanation, though not in a demanding or self-righteous manner. Obviously, *C* is what has happened, and the hidden costs that you failed to take into account were the 12% provincial retail sales tax and 7% federal goods and services tax. Do keep in mind, however, that these hidden costs vary according to each province.

Quiz 7

You have bought a facsimile machine. You bring it home and excitedly plug it in and try to get it working – to no avail. Reading the instruction manual is of no help as it is somewhat technical and you can't understand it. You:

A Bring it back to the store and ask the salesperson to show you how to get it working.

B Ask the salesperson to send someone to your home to show you how to get it working.
C Try to find a friend who knows what he is doing and who will help you to get it working.

Answer

All three answers are possible ways of tackling the problem. If you are fortunate to have such a friend, C is probably the simplest solution. But you are entitled to support from the place where you got the machine. Before doing A, however, it is best to call the store and speak to the person who sold it to you. If it is a reputable store, the salesperson will be helpful. If you choose C or if the salesperson suggests sending someone from the manufacturer's to see you, it is important that you ask whether this service is free. This is to avoid a nasty shock when you receive the bill.

233

Quiz 8

There is something wrong with the lights in your house. You call the electrician and ask him to get to the source of the problem. When he arrives, you:

A Behave business-like, show him the problem and leave him to it.
B Get him a cup of tea and keep up a running commentary about the weather and current events of the week while he works.
C Something between A and B.

Answer

It's all right to adopt a friendly attitude, so something between A and B would be all right. If you choose to do B, be aware that service people often charge you for work done by the hour. The cost of labour and consequently of making a house call to perform a service is expensive. You therefore do not want to waste the repairman's time and your money with inconsequential chatter.

Quiz 9

You have been invited to dinner. When you arrive, you notice that the hostess greets her guests with a hug and a kiss on the cheek. You are uncomfortable, not knowing how to react. You:

A   Pucker up and prepare to hug and kiss too.

B   Resolve to maintain your reserve and decide a handshake is all you will give.

C   Prepare yourself to follow your hostess's lead, and do A or B.

Answer

Canadians come from different backgrounds themselves, and you will find that some are more openly demonstrative than others. If you come from a more reserved tradition, you will feel uncomfortable when everybody around you is effusively demonstrative. The key to how to behave is how well you know your hostess. If you are good friends, A will be acceptable, otherwise a handshake, as suggested in B, will do. If you are uncertain, C is certainly the best thing to do.

Quiz 10

You have gone to another country for a holiday and are talking with some people you have met about the Ontario community in which you now live. One of the people listening to you comments 'I have a Canadian friend who lives in Vancouver now – have you met him by any chance?' You:

A Express surprise that you haven't done so.
B Point out discreetly that it would be unlikely as Vancouver is on the other side of the country from the province of Ontario.
C Realise that the listener has little knowledge of Canadian geography and laugh at him loudly for his ignorance.

Answer

Of course, *B* is the correct answer, as to do *C* would be uncharacteristic of a Canadian, and *A* would certainly reveal your own ignorance of Canadian geography. It is surprising how many people outside Canada don't have any idea of how big Canada actually is, and

that most Canadians know comparatively little about what other parts
of the country are like or about the people who live there.

Quiz 11

Another person listening to you knows that French is an important
language in Canada and comments that you must speak it well as you
have lived in Canada for some years now. You:

A   Say '*oui*', and quickly change the subject before she discovers it
    is just about all the French you know.

B   Explain that even though French is an official language in Canada,
    almost everyone in your community speaks English and that you
    have never had to speak French in order to get along.

C   Explain that it is only in Quebec that French-speakers predomi-
    nate, and thus had you been living in that province, you might have
    learned a little more French.

Answer

You might get away with *A* but it would not increase your friend's understanding of the French-English language situation in Canada. It would be far better to do *B* and *C*.

CULTURE TIPS A–Z

Address Many Canadians have two addresses – their street address and their postal address. The street address is simply where they actually live, e.g. 3355 Panorama Place, and it is the one you would ask for if you were going to visit a friend. The postal address is what you would need if you had to mail something to a friend, and it would be either a 'box number' or an 'RR number', followed by the town, province and postal code.

e.g.   PO Box 123,
        Townsville, Alberta,
        1A2 B3C

or   RR#1, Site 2, Compartment 3,
        Townsville, Alberta,
        1A2 B3C

Alphabet The letters of the alphabet are identified by first names. Those who have been used to saying 'A as in Australia' and 'B as in Bangkok' will now have to change to 'A as in Andrew' and 'B as in Betty' and so on.

Bears There are three species of bears in Canada – the polar bear, grizzly and black or brown bear. Any chance encounters that you might have will probably be with the black bear, as the polar bear is found only on the Arctic coasts and islands, and the grizzly in the south is restricted to the Rocky Mountains of western Alberta and British Columbia. By contrast, the black bear is the most common bear in Canada and can be found almost anywhere. Black bear encounters often occur around campgrounds and other areas, even in small towns in the country, where the bear is trying to get into some food or garbage.

Daylight saving time This comes into effect on the last Sunday in

April when clocks are put forward an hour to take advantage of the longer days. On the last Sunday in October, clocks go back an hour to standard time.

Eh? It is said that Canadians have this habit of tagging 'eh' on to the end of their sentences, as in 'Nice day today, eh?'. While this is true of some Canadians, not all of them speak like this!

Emergencies If you are caught in an emergency and require the services of either the police, fire department or ambulance, the number to dial in most Canadian cities is 911. Many small communities may not have access to the 911 number, in which case, check the front pages of your local telephone directory for the local emergency number to dial.

Family allowance Any resident of Canada who takes care of or supports a child under the age of 18 years is entitled to a family allowance from the federal government.

Flag Although Canadians say they do not openly display their patriotism, there are many who proudly fly their national as well as their provincial flag from a flagpole in their yard.

GST This stands for the federal Goods and Services Tax, which you must pay in addition to the price of any goods or services you purchase. It adds an extra 7% to your bill.

Health insurance There is a national health insurance programme that provides insured health care services to all Canadian residents. Although it is national in scope, it is run by each province and territory, and therefore varies. To be eligible for health insurance benefits, you must register in the province or territory where you are living. In addition, some private insurance companies provide special coverage for newcomers and visitors who are not eligible to register with the provincial schemes.

Identification Your driver's licence is an important and useful piece of document as you will often be asked to produce it as a form of identification, for example when you wish to rent a video cassette tape. Teenagers who are too young to have a driver's licence often use their student's card instead for identification purposes.

Modern conveniences and luxuries The Canadian home is seldom without a clothes washer and dryer (so important when winter makes line drying impossible) in the laundry area, a microwave oven and dishwasher in the kitchen, at least one television set, radio and amplifier in the living room, a telephone and an extension or two in the bedroom.

Money Canadian currency is counted in dollars and cents. The coins consist of the one-cent, five-cent, 10-cent, 25-cent and one-dollar denominations. These are colloquially referred to as the penny, nickle, dime, quarter and loonie (so called because it bears the picture of a loon). The blue one-dollar note is being phased out in favour of the loonie. The commonly used notes come in denominations of C$2, C$5, C$10 and C$20.

Motto Canada's motto is 'From sea to sea', an extract from the Latin version of verse 8 of the 72nd Psalm – 'He shall have dominion also from sea to sea, and from the river unto the ends of the earth.'

Mounties The world-famous Mounties are known as the RCMP or Royal Canadian Mounted Police. Established in 1873 for service in the Northwest, it has now become a federal civilian police force. It is the provincial police force in eight of the 10 provinces – Ontario and Quebec have their own provincial police – and the police force in about 160 municipalities. It also acts as the territorial police force in the North. The official motto of the RCMP is the French phrase '*Maintiens le droit*' or 'Uphold the right'. But the rest of the world has always associated the Mounties with the words 'They always get their man'.

Names A Canadian's family name or surname is often called his last name and his own or given name is referred to as his first name.

Natives Canada's first inhabitants, today they comprise less than 1% of the total population. They are classified as Indian (made up of many bands), Inuit, Dene and Métis. Most of them live on reserves found in every province and territory except for Newfoundland.

O Canada This is Canada's national anthem, and you might want to learn it, even though many Canadians are themselves unsure of the lyrics!:

'O Canada, our home and native land,

True patriot love, in all thy sons command.

With glowing hearts we see thee rise,

The True North strong and free.

From far and wide, O Canada, we stand on guard for thee.

God keep our land glorious and free,

O Canada, we stand on guard for thee,

O Canada, we stand on guard for thee.'

Queue When going shopping or waiting to be served at a counter, Canadians habitually form a queue that is sometimes obvious but at other times invisible. You are expected to take note of those who have come ahead of you and to wait your turn to be served.

Sales tax This is a retail sales tax levied on most goods purchased and it varies from province to province. Newfoundland has the highest sales tax of 12%, followed by New Brunswick (11%), Nova Scotia and Prince Edward Island (10%), Ontario and Quebec (8%), Sasketchewan (7%) and British Columbia (6%). There is no sales tax in Alberta. There may be other factors that determine whether the tax is applied or not. For example, in British Columbia, clothing for children under 16 years and grocery items are exempt from this tax, so it is worth your while to ask.

Social insurance number The social insurance number, or SIN for short, is issued to every taxpayer, using a nine-digit numbering system. A SIN number looks something like this: 737 911 595. It is one of the first things you have to apply for when you come to live in Canada. It is required information when you wish to do something official like applying for a job, claiming unemployment insurance, joining a medical plan or pension fund, or paying income tax. The first digit identifies one of five regional registration offices (1 is Atlantic, 2 Quebec, 4 Ontario, 6 Prairies and 7

Pacific). The final digit is a check number, and the seven middle digits identify the individual holder. The system permits 99 million combinations.

Stamps Postal services are available at post offices or at postal agencies in some stores or shopping centres. It costs 40 cents for the first ounce to mail a letter to any place in Canada, 47 cents to the US, and 80 cents anywhere else overseas. And don't forget, you will be charged another 7% GST!

Store times and business hours Most stores and businesses are open from 9 a.m. to 5 p.m., while drug stores or pharmacies, and supermarkets often stay open till 9 p.m. or later. Most stores open on Saturdays and offer 'late-night shopping' one day a week. Offices generally function Mondays to Fridays.

Taboos Two things to remember are: do not ask a person his age and do not ask how much he paid for something he bought unless you are sure he will not be offended. It is bad manners.

Telephone There is no charge for making a local call. To telephone long-distance within Canada and to the United States, Bermuda and the Caribbean, dial '1' followed by the area code and the telephone number. An international call can be dialled direct by using '011' followed by the country and area codes and telephone number. A special '1 + 800 + telephone number' means you can dial long-distance to that number without charge. Many companies provide this toll-free service for their customers.

Time zones There are six time zones in Canada: Pacific Standard Time (Yukon and most of British Columbia), Mountain Std Time (Alberta, parts of BC, the western half of Sasketchewan, the Mackenzie district or western half of Northwest Territories), Central Std Time (the eastern half of Sasketchewan, Manitoba, that part of Ontario west of Lake Superior, the Keewatin district of NWT), Eastern Std Time (the rest of Ontario, and the western half of Quebec, the Franklin district of NWT), Atlantic Std Time (the rest of Quebec, Nova Scotia, New Brunswick, Prince Edward

Island, the Labrador portion of Newfoundland), and Newfoundland Std Time (the island of Newfoundland). The time difference
between one time zone and the next is an hour except for that
between the Atlantic and Newfoundland times, which is half an
hour. The maximum time difference is that between Pacific and
Newfoundland Std Time, which is four and a half hours.

Voltage Electricity for lights, radio, television and most other
household appliances is supplied at 110 volts. However, some big
electrical appliances such as clothes dryers and electric stoves use
240 volts.

The Weather Network When living in Canada, you quickly learn to
tune in to the Weather Network on television to keep abreast of
weather conditions. The station runs 24 hours a day. Through it,
you will learn to decode the language of warm and cold fronts,
high and low pressure systems, arctic fronts and wind-chill factor.
You won't leave home or plan a trip without first checking with
the Weather Network, as it will tell you what the road conditions
are like. If you are a sailor, it will give you wind and wave
conditions too. A skier? Snow conditions at big ski resorts.

Wind-chill factor The weatherman has a formula for working it out,
but it is sufficient to know that when there is a wind blowing, it can
make the effective temperature of the air fall much lower than the
reading on the thermometer. Practically speaking, although it
might be -20° C on the thermometer, the temperature you actually
experience might be something in the region of -30° C!

BIBLIOGRAPHY

About Canada

To Everything There Is A Season. Roloff Beny, Longmans, 1967. Stunning photographs of Canada accompanied by poems and writings. Originally published to celebrate Canada's centennial year.

Why We Act Like Canadians. Pierre Berton, McClelland and Stewart, 1982. An interesting attempt to explain what being Canadian means, and how the Canadian lifestyle differs from that of the Americans.

The Centennial Food Guide, A Century Of Good Eating. Pierre and Janet Berton, Centennial Publishing Co., 1966. A classic, informative and enjoyable.

Canadian Encyclopaedia, 2nd ed. Hurtig, 1988. An expensive book, but packed full of up-to-date and useful information.

Canadian World Almanac And Book Of Facts. Global Press, annual. The facts and figures about almost everything in Canada.

1001 Questions About Canada. John R. Colombo, Doubleday, 1986. Written by one of Canada's foremost popular statisticians, this book answers common – and some uncommon – questions about Canada.

The Big Picture, What Canadians Think About Almost Everything. Allan R. Gregg, Macfarlane, Walter and Ross, 1990. An insight into the directions that Canada might take in the decade to come.

The Unfinished Country. Bruce Hutchinson, Douglas and McIntyre, 1985. The book probes the development of Canada's political institutions and reveals much of what makes the country operate in the way it does.

Reader's Digest Canadian Book Of The Road. Reader's Digest, 1991. Indispensable for anyone planning a road tour of Canada.

The Canadians. George Woodcock, Fitzhenry and Whiteside, 1979. Some very insightful observations from a man who has made the study of Canada and Canadians his life's work.

Canadian Literature

Margaret Atwood: *Lady Oracle* (1966), *The Handmaid's Tale* (1985) and *Cat's Eye* (1988).

Morley Callaghan: *Our Lady Of The Snows* (1985), *A Wild Old Man On The Road* (1988).

Margaret Laurence: *The Stone Angel* (1964), *A Jest of God* (1966), *The Diviners* (1974).

Stephen Leacock: *Sunshine Sketches Of A Little Town* (1912).

W.O. Mitchell: *Who Has Seen The Wind?* (1947).

Hugh MacLennan: *Two Solitudes* (1945) and *Voices In Time* (1980).

Lucy M. Montgomery: *Anne of Green Gables* (1908).

Farley Mowat: *Never Cry Wolf* (1963) and *A Whale For The Killing* (1972).

Mordecai Richler: *The Apprenticeship Of Duddy Kravitz* (1959), *Joshua Then And Now* (1980) and *Solomon Gursky Was Here* (1989).

Robert Service: *Songs Of A Sourdough* (1907).

Culture Shock

Do's and Taboos Around The World. Roger E. Axtell, John Wiley and Company, 1985.

Beyond Culture. E.T. Hall, Doubleday, 1976.

Survival Kit For Overseas Living. Robert Kohls, Intercultural Press, 1984.

In Another Dimension (A Guide For Women Living Overseas). Nancy Piet-Pelon and Barbara Hornby, Intercultural Press, 1984.

General

Seasons of Canada. Val Clery, Hounslow Press, 1979.

Mysterious Canada. John R. Colombo, Doubleday, 1988.

A Concise Dictionary Of Canadianisms. Gage Educational Publishing, 1973.

Being Canadian. Department of the Secretary of State for Canada, 1988.

The Search For Identity. James Foley (ed.), McMillan, 1976.

Fodor's Guide To Canada 1990. David Mackay Company.

The Unknown Country: Canada And Her People. Bruce Hutchinson, 1977.

Canada, A Travel Survival Kit. Mark Lightbody, Lonely Planet, 1989.

The Canadians. Andrew Malcolm, Times Books, 1985.

Quick Canadian Facts. Canex Enterprises, annual.

The Canadians, How They Live And Work. Jessie and Wreford Watson, Griffin Press, 1977.

Geography

Cultural Patterns In Geography. Gary Birchall, Holt, Rinehart and Winston, 1989.

Investigating Canada. Graham Draper, Irwin, 1990.

Canada, A New Geography. Ralph R. Krueger, Holt, Rinehart, Winston, 1974.

Hinterland And Heartland, A Geography Of Canada. L.D. McCann, Prentice-Hall, 1987.

The Historical Geography Of Canada. Thomas Rumney, Vance Bibliographies, 1985.

History

My Country, The Remarkable Past. Pierre Berton, McClelland and Stewart, 1976.

The National Dream. Pierre Berton, McClelland and Stewart, 1971.

The Illustrated History Of Canada. Craig Brown (ed.), Lester and Orphen Dennys, 1987.

Pioneer Days In Upper Canada. Edwin C. Guillet, University of Toronto Press, 1973.

A Short History Of Canada. D.C. Masters, Van Nostrand Company, 1958.

True Blue: The Loyalist Legend. Walter Stewart, Collins, 1985.

Government, Law and Politics
Civil Rights, The Law And You. P. Michael Bolton, Self Counsel Press, 1989.
Ethnicity And Human Rights In Canada. Evelyn Kallen , Gale, 1982.
Immigrating To Canada, How To Do It. Gary Segal, Self-counsel Press, 1990.

Family and Society
The Emerging Generation: An Inside Look At Canada's Teenagers. Reginald Bibby, 1985.
Canada–Charter Equality Rights For Women; One Step Forward Or Two Steps Back? Gwen Brodsky, Canadian Advisory Council on the Status of Women, 1989.
Indians Of Canada. Diamond Jenness, University of Toronto Press, 1977.
I Am An Indian. Kent Gooderham, J.M. Dent, 1969.
The Canadian Mother And Child. Health and Welfare Canada, Douglas and McIntyre, 1979.
Towns And Villages In Canada: The Importance Of Being Unimportant. Gerald Hodge and Mohammed A. Qaheen, Butterworths, 1983.
Canada; Immigrants And Settlers. Ian Hundly, Gage, 1980.
The Canadian Family; A Book Of Readings. Karigouder Ishwaran (ed.), Gage, 1983.
Just Looking, Thank You: An Amused Observer's View Of Canadian Lifestyles. Philip Marchand, MacMillan, 1976.
Urban Sociology In Canada. Peter McGahan, Butterworths, 1986.
Sexual Politics. Kate Millet, Simon and Schuster, 1990.
The Changing People. Palmer and Mary Lou Paterson, Collier-McMillan, 1971.
Multi-Culturalism In Canada. Ronald J. Samuda et al, Allyn and Bacon, 1984.
Canada's Seniors: A Dynamic Force. Statistics Canada, 1988.
The Seniors Boom, Dramatic Increases In Longevity And Prospects

For Better Health. Leroy O. Stone, Statistics Canada, 1986.

The Vertical Mosaic. John Porter, University of Toronto Press, 1968.

Canadian Women, A History. Alison Prentice et al, Harcourt, Brace and Jovanovich, 1988.

Drug Alert, A Provocative Look At Street Drugs. Marilu Weissman, J. Wiley and Sons, 1979.

Canadian Culture

Harness In The Parlor: A Book Of Early Canadian Facts And Folklore. Audrey Armstrong, Musson, 1977.

Editing Canadian English. Douglas and McIntyre, 1987.

Divisions On A Ground: Essays On Canadian Culture. Northrop Frye, Awasi Press, 1982.

Our Own Voice, Canadian English And How It Came To Be. Ruth E. McConnel, Gage, 1978.

A Reader's Guide To The Canadian Novel. John Moss, McClelland and Stewart, 1987.

Modern Canadian English Usage. M. H. Scargill, McClelland and Stewart, 1974.

Dictionary of Newfoundland English. G.M. Story *et al*, University of Toronto Press, 1982.

Doing Business in Canada

Starting A Business. Gordon Brockhouse, 1989.

The complete Canadian Small Business Guide. Douglas A. Gray, McGraw Hill and Ryerson, 1988.

The Financial Post 100 Best Companies To Work For In Canada. Eva Innes, 1990.

Food and Entertainment

The Canadian Guide To Home Entertaining. Una Abrahamson, Clarke Irwin, 1975.

150 Classic Canadian Recipes. Elizabeth Baird, Lorimer, 1974.

The Canadian Cookbook: A Complete Heritage Of Canadian Cooking. Jehane Benoit, Pagurian Press, 1970.

Pierre and Janet Berton's Canadian Food Guide. Pierre Berton, 1974.

The Châtelaine Cookbook. Elaine Collett, *Châtelaine* magazine, 1973.

Provincial Cooking Of Canada. Culinary Arts Institute, Delair Publishing, 1983.

The Canadian Living Entertaining Cookbook. Carol Ferguson, 1990.

Canadian Family Cooking. Norman Kolpas, Footnote Productions, 1986.

Sports and Recreation

Bright Waters, Bright Fish: An Examination Of Angling In Canada. Roderick L. Haig-Brown, Douglas and McIntyre, 1985.

A Guide to Hunting In North America. Jerome J. Knap, Pagurian Press, 1975.

One Hundred Years of Hockey. Brian McFarlane, Deneau, 1989.

Canoeing Ontario's Rivers. Ron Reid, Douglas and McIntyre, 1985.

THE AUTHORS

Born in England, **Robert Barlas** has always had the wanderlust in his veins. At the age of 19, he migrated to Canada, which has been his home – on and off – for the last 25 years.

A teacher, Bob has made a career out of working in international education all over the world. Among the countries he has worked in are England, New Zealand, Singapore, the People's Republic of China and Sri Lanka. Bob and his family made many friends in Sri Lanka and he co-authored *Culture Shock! Sri Lanka*. The Barlases have been back in Canada since 1989.

Bob enjoys reading, writing, skiing and sailing, and, of course, travelling, which has taken him and most of his family to over 60 countries so far – the rest of the world he is still working on!

Pang Guek Cheng was born in Singapore into a large Peranakan (Straits-born Chinese) family. She received her education in Singapore and was a journalist and sub-editor with the *Straits Times* for 13 years. She also tried her hand at book editing for a few years. After having written articles for magazines and newspapers, it is a natural progression for her to write books now.

Guek Cheng has travelled widely. The places she has *not* been to are South America, China, Africa and Greenland. She believes in travelling as a mind-broadening experience. She has lived in England for one year, and is now a permanent resident of British Columbia, Canada, together with her husband and two children.

Guek Cheng loves reading, music, travelling and playing tennis. She has also taken up cross-country skiing, a popular pastime in Canada.

INDEX